Developing Bots

with

Selenium Python

for

Web Scraping,

Test Engineering, Data Mining,

and Automation

FIRST EDITION

Developing Bots
with
Selenium Python

~ for ~

Web Scraping, Test Engineering, Data Mining, and Automation

~ by ~

Michael Schrenk

Published by
Mepso Media LLC, Nevada USA
www.mepso.com
First Edition October 2023

Developing Bots with Selenium Python

© 2023 Michael Schrenk

ISBN: 979-8-9887623-1-7

Please contact the publisher as shown below for:

- Permission requests,
- Interview requests,
- Review copies, or
- Speaker inquiries.

Mepso Media LLC
4952 S Rainbow Boulevard, #702
Las Vegas NV 89118
Attention: Permissions Coordinator

www.mepso.com

In loving memory

Charlotte Schrenk
1897-1982

Table of Contents

About the author

Michael Schrenk leverages twenty-five years of bot development experience and decades of data analysis to create truly competitive advantages for clients. This—his third book on the topic, joins his first two books, "Webbots, Spiders, and Screen Scrapers" (No Starch Press, 1st and 2nd Edition, 2007 and 2012), which were declared by Dr. Dobbs Journal as *"The definitive introduction to the topic"*. He is a sought after speaker and has presented talks everywhere from Moscow to Silicon Valley and is a nine-time speaker at the notorious DEF CON hacking convention.

Figure 0, Michael Schrenk at the National Palace of Culture, Sofia Bulgaria

Mike spent his early career, in Minneapolis Minnesota. And after taking a few years to focus on international clients, he settled in the beautiful American Southwest where he currently lives with his wife Paula, and their long-haired Chihuahua, Cali[1].

Apart from writing and technology, Mike is also a *LBC*, or Little British Car, enthusiast and enjoys long-scale guitars and single-coil neck pick-ups.

---

1   Not his password, sorry. :-)

Acknowledgments

I want to extend a heartfelt apology to both Paula my wife, and to my Chihuahua Cali. I need to apologize for the missed walks, early evenings, late nights, and the random middle-of-the-night grammar questions. (I'll leave it to you to decide who deserves which apologies.)

Section I: Introduction

Using the techniques in this book, there is no website that you can't scrape, test, or automate. Any website! This means you'll be able to tackle a wide variety of projects, ranging from:

- Test Engineering (of online services),
- Automation of routine online tasks,
- Competitive Intelligence,
- Data Journalism,
- Data (intelligence) collection, and
- Operational Security (OpSec),

CHAPTER 1, WHY WRITE A BOT?

Bot development has changed significantly since the publication of my last book[2], in 2012, but the reasons for writing bots are largely the same. And after more than a decade since that book, business and organizations still use bots as the primary way to facilitate connection to, and automation of, the Internet.

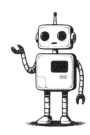

Why a Selenium bot?

Selenium has become the number one tool in many bot developer's arsenal—certainly in mine! This is because Selenium solves the problems caused by changing trends in web design techiques. Those changes were primarily the increase in the number of websites and web applications that relied on *Active Content*. Active Content refers to any web content that is obtained without a page reflow. In other words, after a web page is initially downloaded, additional data, and or controls, can be summoned from the server, and rendered on the web page, without reflowing the web page. This extra communication is accomplished though JavaScript and a technology called AJAX. We'll talk about AJAX in detail in Chapter 6, but for now, know that the technology that facilitates today's engaging features, like endless scrolling and predictive search, cause real headaches for bot developers using traditional methods because old techniques are blind to any data that's downloaded after the initial page flow. Selenium, in contrast, has no problem reading the contents of a web page at anytime and is the easy answer to the problem of active content.

What is Selenium?

Selenium interfaces to web browsers through some magic called Webdriver (Chapter 17). Selenium is not a language, but a browser interface that must be controlled by another language, usually Python, Java, or C++, though there are also lesser used

---

2   Schrenk, M. (2012). Webbots, spiders, and screen scrapers: A guide to developing internet agents with PHP/curl (2nd ed.). No Starch Press.

Selenium packages for Ruby and a few others. And while I haven't personally seen them all, I can say that the Selenium interfaces for Python and Java are quite similar, but not quite identical. Both versions of Selenium, Python and Java, have many similarities to JavaScript—largely because of their use of DOM, or the Document Object Model.

Why Python?

Selenium is only an interface into a browser environment. You still needs a computer program to control it and to interface Selenium to the resources required by modern bots. The choice of computer language often comes down to a combination of personal preference and circumstance. And that was certainly my situation when I selected Python as a Selenium control language. When I chose Python instead of Java, it wasn't because I believed that Java was a bad choice. It was because I already had quite a bit of Java experience and it felt like a good time to learn Python. That's why I initially chose Python. But you can do the same things with either language.

What is a bot?

The bots described in this book have been given a number of names since I started writing bots in the '90s. For example, those programs that perform searches for search engines used to be called "crawlers", "worms", or "spiders", for the way the metaphorically moved and self-discovered their way through the Internet. Now they're just called bots; as are the programs that I used to refer to as "Webbots" or "Screen Scrapers". They're all just bots now.

While chatbots aren't new, *AI,* or Artificial Intelligence, powered chatbots are. But as this book focuses on: Web Scraping, Test Engineering, Data Mining, and Automation, chatbots aren't specifically mentioned after this point. Though you could certainly use the tools in this book to interface another program to any web-based AI chatbot. Selenium has your back.

What do people do with bots?

The most numerous bots are those that are those that work behind the scenes testing websites, web applications, phone apps, and datasets. Because the biggest use for Selenium—by far, is for Test Engineering.

But there are many other things that developers can do with Selenium Python other than Test Engineering. Personally, I've primarily developed bots for non-test purposes, mostly in Competitive Intelligence Campaigns. These bots range from single-desktop bots that run one time to swarms of bots in the cloud that work together as a team and run continually for months on end. Those bots were primarily used in retail situations, where market data is used to calculate prices and inventory needs.

Figure 1.1, DEF CON 21, How my Botnet Purchased Millions of Dollars in Cars.

One of my bots purchased a couple million dollars in underpriced cars over a nine month periods[3]. That was probably the most fun I ever had, not just as a bot developer, but as a software developer in general. this talk was also included in the list of the Top Ten DEF CON talks of all time[4].

I've written bots to assist law enforcement with the management of criminals. I've written bots for foreign governments. I even wrote a bot to help catch an identity impersonator on MySpace—a long, long, time ago.

---

3 YouTube. (2013, November 16). *Defcon 21 - how my botnet purchased millions of dollars in cars and defeated the Russian hackers.* YouTube. https://www.youtube.com/watch?v=sgz5dutPF8M

4 *The best DEF CON talks of all time!.* InfoSec Conferences. (2022, November 30). https://infosec-conferences.com/best-def-con-talks/

My first bots

My first bots were designed to connect heart patients, in some of the most remote parts of Canada, with Cardiologist at major Heart Centers. At the time, remote *EKGs*, or electrocardiograms, where collected by machines of he same name and then either faxed to the specialist for interpretation, or they were connected live through a MODEM-like device. Neither solutions were great because they required a patient to travel to the doctor, and the quality of the electrocardiograms was poor. In response to this situation, my first bot used Java, and a Browser Applet to connect a patient in their home to a specialist with the use of a disposable, self-applied monitor. This bot allowed the doctor to talk with, and view a video of, the patient while reading their live their EKG.

In later years bot's, and bot development, have taken me all over Eastern and Western Europe, North Africa, and the near entirety of North America. One of the nice things about bot development is that there are enough niches to satisfy nearly anyone's interests. Bot have taken me to places I never thought I'd go, like teaching bot technologies to European Investigative Journalists, or speaking live on BBC World Service to an audience of millions.

Fortunately, each of these very different bots were developed with essentially the same skill set.

What about the naughty bots?

I knew this would come-up. So we may as well cover this issue now. Yes, there are many bots that are written to commit crimes. That's because bots interface with the Internet, and if you're going to commit Internet crime—at scale, it only makes sense that criminals would write crimeBots. These naughty bots can commit all kinds of crimes, ranging from changing prices on online stores, to commuting identity theft, to debiting micropayments from thousands of bank accounts.

Fortunately, bots can also do a lot of good. And there is an entire industry to support legitimate bot development. Unfortunately, the skills to write good bots are the same skills that write naughty bots. But you can't let a few crooks spoil the game for everyone.

How does the saying go? "Once you criminalize bots, only criminals will have bots."

What parts of Selenium does this book cover?

Selenium is a suite of tools that allow for online testing, data collection, and automation. And while each of the parts of the suite are important, this book primarily deals with the software known as *Selenium Webdriver*, or just Webdriver. The other aspects of Selenium, including: Selenium RC, Selenium IDE, and Selenium Grid are less important from this book's perspective. But they are also described here for completeness, and so you can sound "interesting" at your next cocktail party. :-)

Selenium Webdriver

Selenium Webdriver is the focus of this book, and the current standard and most widely used version of Selenium. It provides a programming interface that enables users to interact with web browsers directly using programming languages such as Java, Python, C#, etc. Webdriver allows developers to write more powerful and flexible test scripts by utilizing programming constructs and libraries. It provides control over browser interactions, element identification, and handling complex scenarios.

Selenium RC (Remote Control)

Selenium RC was the initial version of Selenium that allowed users to interact with web browsers using a JavaScript-based automation framework. It worked by injecting JavaScript into the browser to automate interactions. Selenium RC is now considered deprecated and has been replaced by Webdriver.

Selenium IDE (Integrated Development Environment)

Selenium IDE is a browser extension that provides a browser-based "record-and-playback" functionality that creates Selenium Python scripts based on interactions with the browser while in record mode. Selenium IDE is intended to be useful for quick test script creation but has limited capabilities compared to Webdriver. While the IDE sounds promising, in practice, I have found little use for it. So, it will not be a focus of this book.

Selenium Grid

Selenium Grid is a component of Selenium that allows the parallel execution of scripts across multiple machines and browsers. It enables distributed testing using a hub and multiple nodes, where each node represents a different browser and operating system combination. With Selenium Grid, you can distribute tests across these nodes, which can significantly speed up the testing process and improve efficiency. Selenium Grid is beyond the scope of this book.

CHAPTER 2, BOOK FEATURES

This book actually represents a collection of media including the book, projects (code), target web pages, and a collection of videos.

Example bot projects

We begin this chapter by introducing a variety of example bot projects. These projects will provide practical illustrations, demonstrating how bots can automate tasks, collect data, and engage with web applications. These examples cover activities such as web scraping and CAPTCHA solving with hopes of sparking your own creativity and to motivate you to develop customized bots that align with your particular requirements. These illustrative projects are designed to showcase Selenium functionality while focusing on those aspects that you are most apt to use.

Also sprinkled throughout this book are a collection of "ProTip!" callouts that feature related anecdotes and industry. These feature a range of topics from parsing to encounters with the FBI.

The projects in this book include:

1. A Minimal Viable Selenium Product, to verify your environment,

2. The advantages to using a botDev framework,

3. A look at how Selenium manages Active Content (AJAX),

4. A procurement project (a bot that buys cups),

5. Using ActionChains to control a set of JQuery controls

6. A tutorial on collecting and aggregation data from various sources,

7. A simple regression test,

8. How to solve CAPTCHAs,

9. Developing a bot that plays games, and

10. Running Selenium in headless (browser-less) mode.

The intent of these examples is to get you up and running as quickly as possible while referring to *Section III, Theory,* for more detailed explanations of specific industry knowledge and thorough histories.

YouTube demonstrations & code walk-throughs

In addition to this book, you also have access to a set of links to a selection of YouTube videos that provide code walk-throughs and bot demonstrations. These videos are a supplement to this book and offer valuable insights into the code implementation process, making it easier for you to grasp the concepts and techniques behind successful bot development.

 The comment sections of these videos will also contain updates from the author, and room for your to ask your questions or make your comments.

Figure 2.1, Look for this symbol to find links to related videos

Be sure to watch the comment sections of the videos for this book on YouTube for updates, and a place for you to raise questions and contact the author.

Each of these YouTube videos contain:

- Design notes,

- A personally narrated code walk-through, and

- A video of the bot in operation.

Test websites = a safe place to practice

Each of the examples in this book is accompanied by at least one private test website that was developed specifically for this book. The reasons for these test websites are twofold:

1. Creating specific websites for this book ensure that your environment doesn't change after this book is published,

2. These websites are a safe place to fail. For example, you can order products from our online store without committing your self to an actual order. You can also make mistakes without jeopardizing the performance of an actual website or worrying about violating a website's Terms of Service.

Script libraries

Compiling an extensive array of pre-constructed tools and assets is vital for streamlining bot development. In the script section, we will delve into a range of script libraries crafted with bot development in mind. These libraries provide readily available functions, modules that simplify intricate tasks and expedite your progress in bot development.

The scripts are also available for download at the book's web page, which can be found at www.mepso.com.

CHAPTER 3, CONFIGURATION

One way to learn a technology is to configure your own development environment. This book will attempt to guide you through the process of configuration your development environment. In learning to set-up your own machine, you'll learn how to configure other computers. And, you'll be better equipped to debug your code when you better understand your environment.

Platforms

Selenium and Python are fairly platform independent, so developers have a lot of options when it comes to establishing development, test, and production environments. The ability to span environments is a powerful thing, as projects often require more than one environment to be effective.

For example, my personal development environment is primarily Mac-based, because of similarities to the Unix-like LAMP environments I've been working in for the past twenty-five years. But with Selenium Python, I typically develop on Windows instances hosted in *AWS*, or Amazon Web Services. I then access the remote Windows box from a Mac via *Microsoft Remote Desktop.* I choose a cloud-based approach because it is cheap and universally available. And, I love the flexibility of developing from my Macbook or my full-blown desk set-up with a 43" monitor. It's also an advantage to be able to access my bots from an iPad or even my phone.

Once the bot is debugged, I'll often deploy on a cheaper Linux instance (also in AWS). Of course, to use Selenium Python in a non-windowed environment means converting the application to *Headless Mode*, which is something you'll read about in Chapter 13.

You can also develop Selenium Python programs on a windowed Linux environment, like Ubuntu Linux, however, it's not covered in this book. But the process would be the same.

Hardware

You don't need exotic hardware to learn Selenium Python or to use any of the example bots in this book. A reasonably modern, functional, PC or Macintosh with Internet access is all you really need. Again, if you're using a Linux-based computer , your configuration will be similar to that of a Mac.

Installing Python

Python installation instructions are available at `www.python.org`. There you can find installation packages for various operating systems. This official Python website also offers insights on installation as well.

In my case, Python was part of the original software installations found in both my PC and Mac environments. So, before you install Python, first check if it is already installed. You can do this by typing the following.

```
%> python --version
Python 3.11.3
```

Script 3.1, Determining the Python version

It is not uncommon for both Python 2 and Python 3 to be loaded on the same computer. So instead of typing "python" in the example in Script 3.1, you may have to type "python2" or "python3" to get the correct interpreter to run. Sometimes, python is also simply abbreviated as "py".

> For consistency, this book will always execute Python programs with the "python" instruction.

The Python scripts referenced by this book were all written in Python 3. If you're still using Python 2, this would be a good time to upgrade as there have been significant changes between versions 2 and 3. Additionally, Python 2 was *sunsetted*, or put to rest on January 1, 2020 and is no longer supported.

Installing Pip

After installing Python, you will want to verify that Pip is installed. Pip is the de facto package manager for Python is installed. Pip streamlines the process of installing and managing Python libraries and packages from the Python Package Index (PyPI), a repository that contains thousands of third-party packages.

While it's clear that Pip is an acronym, it is less clear what 'PIP' stands for. I've heard both "Python Installer Package" and "Pip Installs Packages".

Pip is installed via python on a command line, as shown below.

```
$ python -m pip install --upgrade pip
```

Script: 3.2, Installing pip.

Pip is a very important part of python development as Pip allows developers to quickly and easily install packages by automating the process of downloading, checking version dependencies, building, and installing the necessary files.

Pip also allows developers to specify and manage the version of packages they're using in their projects, ensuring compatibility and reducing the risk of issues due to version conflicts.

Using pip

Once pip is installed, it can be used to perform a number of code package related tasks, as shown below in Figure 3.1.

The format for using pip is: "pip command package-name". Listed below are examples of a variety of things you might do with pip.

Function	Syntax
Install a package	`pip install package-name`
Install a package with a specific version number	`pip install package-name==version`
Upgrade a package to the latest version	`pip install -upgrade package-name`
Uninstall a package	`pip uninstall package-name`
Search for a package	`pip search package-name`
Show package details	`pip show package-name`

Figure 3.1, Examples of how pip is used to install, uninstall, search for, and show packages.

In summary, pip is a crucial tool for Python developers, as it simplifies the process of installing and updating third-party packages. By leveraging the extensive library of third-party packages available; developers can accelerate development and improve the quality of code.

Installing Selenium

Once pip is installed you can install the Selenium library with Pip. Selenium is installed with the following line.

```
$ pip install selenium
```

Script: 3.3, Installing selenium

Once the command from the above script is entered, Pip will install Selenium and satisfy any unresolved dependencies.

Downloading Webdriver/Chromedriver

The last of the basic configurations is setting-up Webdriver. Webdriver is the software that interfaces Selenium to the browser. There are versions of Webdriver for interfacing to most popular browsers. Your selection of browser will determine which version of Webdriver you need as the browser and Webdriver must match. The ability to switch between client agents is incredibly useful for engineers testing browser compatibility in web pages. A single bot could control both a Chrome browser and a copy of Microsoft Edge if it loaded both Webdrivers and drove two browsers. This ability makes version compatibility tests relatively easy to construct.

And while it can be incredibly useful to be able to switch control between multiple browsers, we are going to limit our exploration to the Chrome browser and to the user of Chromedriver for simplicity. Additionally, we'll be using the Chrome Inspect tool later in this book.

So when you see the word Webdriver mentioned in this book, assume we're talking about Chromedriver.

> This book focuses exclusively on the Chromedriver version of Webdriver.

Once Selenium is installed we can begin writing Selenium Python programs. But there are a few aspects of Webdriver that need to be addressed first.

Webdriver / Browser revision issues

One of the issues you'll soon discover is that the version of Webdriver must match the browser version level. You'll want to start with the most current version of both your Chrome browser and Chromedriver. So, before you download Chromedriver, be sure that: your Chrome browser is at the latest version. This is easily done with the following:

1. Open Chrome and click on the three dot menu on the upper right corner of the Chrome screen.

2. At the bottom of the resulting menu, click on "Help", and finally

3. Click on "About Google Chrome.

If your Chrome browser isn't at the current version, it will either automatically begin to download the latest stable version, or tell you that your browser is out of date. In either case, it's a good idea to start with the current revision.

At `chromedriver.chromium.org/downloads,` you'll find Chromedriver installation packages for various revisions and platforms. You will probably always want the very latest version, as that's the one that will interface properly with the most recent version of Chrome.

Your Chromedriver download will probably arrive in a zip compressed folder. I like to put the unzipped version in my development directory, a directory below my development directory. This allows multiple bots, from different projects, to all use the same Chromedriver. This also simplifies Chromedriver version management.

In my experience, Chromedriver needs to be updated every two or three months, in coordination with Chrome browser updates. It's hard to stay on top of synchronizing the versions of Chrome and Chromedriver because Chrome is apt to update itself without your knowledge. In my experience, there is no reliable way to keep Chrome from updating itself. You'll know when you have a versioning issue when you attempt to run your bot and it fails because the installed Webdriver can't load the browser.

Final Chromedriver configuration

Once you've unzipped the Webdriver executable, and located it within your bot environment, there are two more things you need to do before your done with the install (actually three if you're using a Mac.)

Chromedriver must be in the system path

You need to ensure that Webdriver is in your system path definitions. If you're on a PC, that means finding the *PATH variable* in the system configurations and adding the path to your Webdriver in to PATH (in the laughably small text box). If you're using a MAC (or a Linux alternative) you can simply type the following at a command prompt.

```
# SETTING PATH VARIABLE ON A MAC
export PATH=$PATH:/absolute/path/to/Chromedriver/
```

Script 3.4, Setting system path variable on a Mac

Webdriver must be executable

The next step is to ensure that the file permissions ensure that Webdriver is executable. If you're using a PC, simply use File Explorer to locate the file and "right mouse click" on the Webdriver and follow the onscreen instructions for setting the file to executable, as shown below.

Figure 3.2, Configuring Windows file permissions

If you are using a Mac, or a Linux-based computer, navigate to the directory that Webdriver is in and type the command from Script 3.5.

```
chmod +x chromedriver    # you may need to precede with a sudo command
```

Script 3.5, Setting Chromedriver (Webdriver) permissions to executable on a Mac

You might need to "jailbreak" Webdriver (Mac only)

If you're using Mac, your operating system will not run unapproved programs without your approval, even though the file permissions are set to executable. If you want to run a program that's not on the approved list—like Webdriver, you may have to *Jailbreak*, or tell your computer that it has your permission to run. To ensure that Webdriver can be

39

executed, open a terminal and move into the directory where you placed chromedriver. (The same place you just set in your system path). The run the command below.

```
# MAC ONLY
xattr -d com.apple.quarantine Chromedriver
```

Script 3.6, Jailbreaking Chromedriver on a Mac

This command will take Chromedriver out of quarantine and make it available to your Selenium Python script.

Do I need to install pytest?

Pytest is a popular testing framework for Python that can make writing and organizing tests easier, but it is not mandatory for using Selenium. You will need pytest, however, if you want to run programs created by the Selenium IDE, which was discussed in Section I and not otherwise covered in this book.

Section II: Example projects

This section is designed to get you up, running, and understanding Selenium Python as quickly possible. In this section, we present a carefully curated collection of example projects aimed at helping readers explore the capabilities and potential of Selenium Python. As a powerful web automation framework, Selenium has a wide range of applications, from automating repetitive tasks to extracting data from websites and ensuring web applications function as intended.

The primary focus of the example problems is to provide readers with a diverse set of practical scenarios that highlight specific aspects of Selenium. These problems cover areas such as form completion, web scraping, testing, navigation, interaction with dynamic web elements, and headless operation. By working through these examples, readers will gain hands-on experience with Selenium and understand its applications in real-world contexts.

These example scripts progressively build on each other, allowing you to develop skills and knowledge incrementally. The examples cover both basic and advanced functionalities, ensuring that readers of all levels can benefit from these exercises.

A FEW WORDS ABOUT THE PROJECTS

Here are a few words to help you get the most for these projects.

Special "test" web pages

This book includes access to special "test" or target web pages that are safe places where you to point your bots. This gives you the freedom to practice on web pages that exists for the sole purpose of learning and testing your skills. With these practice webpages, you won't have to worry about violating someones Terms of Service or copyright issues. You can feel free to practice.

Fault tolerance

Most training material is a compromise, and these projects are no exception. To clarify the message, I chose simplicity over robustness in each of these examples. It actually takes a lot to develop a fault tolerant bots, and I believe that a stress on developing "production ready" bots would have become an early distraction from learning Selenium. The fact that you have target web pages, that don't change, is a big part of improving the fault tolerance of these bots. When you target web pages in the wild, you will have fewer guarantees.

Instead of complicating the projects, I decided to write a whole chapter devoted to Fault Tolerance in Section III (Chapter 20, Fault Tolerance). I highly suggest that you read and implement the hints in this chapter before you deploy a bot in a production environment.

Watch the associated videos on YouTube

Don't forget that each of these projects has an associated video on YouTube. These videos had narrated code walk-throughs and bot demos. The YouTube comment sections are also a great place to ask questions, brag about your success, or to contact the author.

LIST OF PROJECTS

1. Hello world

This program demonstrates a minimal Selenium Python script. It only loads Webdriver and ensures that a web page can be loaded. This script has two essential purposes: To show how to load the Webdriver as a service—and more importantly, to verify that the development environment was properly set-up.

2. Framework

While the previous example was useful for demonstrating that you can load a Webdriver and test your development environment, it is not something you'd want to base a production-level bot around. While the word "framework" might be a bit of an exaggeration, it is important to standardize on a set of reusable code to facilitate better performance and quick(er) development. This example framework creates a standard way to: load Webdriver, access standard libraries, and provide logging capability. All subsequent examples use this framework.

3. AJAX and active content

This example shows how Selenium manages Active Content, or Asynchronously Loading Content. This bot interacts with web elements loaded dynamically through AJAX, JavaScript, or other technologies. This exercise will teach readers how to deal with complex web pages that involve asynchronous data loading and user interactions.

4. Automating procurement

This demonstration project uses an online store, especially created for this book, to practice writing a bot that automatically buys items for procurement. This demonstration also shows how to authenticate and gain access to a protected website, place an order, and record a receipt.

5. ActionChains and custom controls

Selenium provides clever scripting options for imitating intricate mouse actions with something called ActionChains. This project will teach your bot how to drag, drop, right click, hover, and more.

6. Parsing and aggregation

This programming example explores various data collection and parsing techniques. It also highlights the value of aggregating irregular data into standardized *CSV*, or Comma Separated Values files. This chapter is a good companion to the chapter on Big Data in Section III.

7. Regression testing

Sometimes, old bugs reappear when production software is updated. These "regressions" need to be found. Here are some automated tools to perform regression tests.

8. Solving CAPTCHAs

There are very legitimate reasons for needing to solve a CAPTCHA. For example, what if you're writing bots that test websites with CAPTCHAs? You're going to need to test (solve) them. This chapter shows the easiest, most sure-proof, approach.

9. Bots that play games

This bot demonstration automatically plays Tic Tak Toe with another computer. This application is also used in the next example, where the program runs in Headless Mode (without a browser).

10. Headless browsing

This example features Selenium's ability to control a web browser without using an actual web browser. There are many reasons why you might want to run Selenium Python without a browser, with the primary reason being easier scaling and cheaper hosting.

## Chapter 4

PROJ 01: HELLO WORLD

Our first bot is probably as small as one can get and still call itself a Selenium Python program. This first bot only loads Selenium, downloads a web page, and exits.

While it may sound small and insignificant, this "Hello World" program is more than an introduction to programming in Selenium Python. It's real purpose is to verify that your development environment is ready for the projects that come next.

How Selenium works (in short)

Before we get too far along, it is good to know the mechanics of what we're doing. So here is a 30,000 foot view of how Selenium Python works.

Selenium is not a language, it is an interface. To get Selenium to do anything, you need a programming language. The most common control languages for Selenium include: Python, Java, and C++. In our case, Python interfaces with Selenium when it loads the Selenium library.

Selenium is an interface into Webdriver, which is what loads and controls the browser. Selenium and Webdriver communicate over a network connection with a protocol called the Webdriver protocol. This granulation provides great flexibility and makes it easy to interface Webdrivers for multiple browsers.

Watch the associated video on YouTube

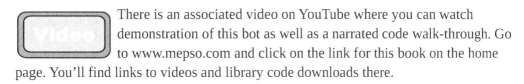 There is an associated video on YouTube where you can watch demonstration of this bot as well as a narrated code walk-through. Go to www.mepso.com and click on the link for this book on the home page. You'll find links to videos and library code downloads there.

Figure 4.1, Link to chapter video

This bot validates your environment

This chapter is a little different than the others in this section, in that this project is more about testing your development environment than actually writing a useful bot. This overly simplified project is also necessary to verify that your paths are correctly set, Selenium is property installed, and that you are able to load and execute your Webdriver. So, this project largely demonstrates that you are ready for more involved projects that come later.

Figure 4.2, Our target, the helloWorld web page

This project is in contrast to the one that follows in the next chapter. That project describes another way to set-up a project for more "industrial use". That project eventually becomes the template that the other bots are derived from. So, since you have that to look forward to, I would limit the use of this project after you're satisfied that it works and it validates that your configuration is good. You have better things ahead.

Code walk-through

The code in this example is quite simple. So, this code description may feel a bit pedantic to some of you (my apologies) but, I can assure you that things will get more complex as we proceed.

Importing libraries

This script starts as any Python script would, with the importation of a few libraries, as shown below.

```
#######################################
# helloWord.py
#######################################

import  sys                     # Import sys so we can use sys.exit()
import  time                    # Import time library
from    selenium import webdriver# Import interface to browser
```

Script 4.1, Importing Python libraries

The three libraries that are imported here are `sys`, `time`, and `Webdriver`. The `sys` library contains things required to manage a Python program. This includes, providing a way to use command line variables, configure local paths, communicate with standard devices, and to exit cleanly from the program. The `time` library holds the time function the bot uses to provide a short delay. From Selenium, we are importing the `Webdriver`, which actually means we are importing access to the Webdriver Protocol, which is something we'll use now and explain further later.

Loading Webdriver

Next, the bot loads the Chromedriver, which determines which browser we'll be emulating as we use the Webdriver protocol, as shown in the figure shown below.

```
# Load webdriver as a service
driver_path = "../../libs/webdrivers/chromedriver"
service = webdriver.chrome.service.Service(executable_path=driver_path)
service.start()
driver = webdriver.Chrome(service=service)

service = Webdriver.chrome.service.Service(executable_path=driver_path)
service.start()


# Now you can create a Webdriver instance using the service object
driver = Webdriver.Chrome(service=service)
```

Script 4.2, Loading Webdriver

The Webdriver service is responsible for handling the browser requests and communicating with the Webdriver libraries, in our case, Chromedriver. This means that all of our bots will look like they are using a Chrome browser. If you have a browser compatibility test need, or would just like to learn about the other flavors of Webdriver, please reference Chapter 17 on Webdriver.

Webdriver is loaded as a service, creating an instance of the Webdriver (Chromedriver, in our case) that runs as a separate process. Though we're not doing it, loading Webdriver in this way facilitates Webdriver to run on a remote machine. This approach is often used for distributed scenarios. If you're interested in bot architectures, you might want to skip ahead to *Chapter 19, "Scaling and Architecture"*.

Load a web page and exit cleanly

The last part of this simple exercise is to load a web page and exist cleanly.

```
# Open a website
driver.get("http://www.mepso.com/helloWorld")

# Wait a moment
time.sleep(10)

# Exit gracefully (This sequence is important.)
driver.close()            # shutdown the browser
driver.quit()             # close driver
sys.exit()                # exit from the program
```

Script 4.3, Exiting gracefully (this sequence is important)

Here, in Script 4.3s, the driver is used to download a web page. Nothing is actually done with the web page, but that's not the point. The point is to see the browser open when Chromedriver loads and accesses the web page.

The chromedriver is then closed "gracefully", by first closing the browser window, and then closing our use of the driver. And finally, the program is closed.

While this program doesn't appear to be very useful, it actually have multiple purposes, including to:

- Show how to load Webdriver,

- Verify that your Webdriver can be loaded (paths and permissions are OK)

- Access the Internet, and

- Close down safely.

More importantly, this example is the seed for a more production-worthy template that will be used throughout the rest of this section.

Full script: helloWorld.py

```
#######################################
# helloWord.py
#######################################

import   sys                  # Import sys so we can use sys.exit()
import   time                 # Import time library
from      selenium import webdriver# Import interface to browser

# Load webdriver as a service
driver_path = "../../libs/webdrivers/chromedriver"
service = webdriver.chrome.service.Service(executable_path=driver_path)
service.start()
driver = webdriver.Chrome(service=service)

# Open a website
driver.get("http://www.mepso.com/helloWorld")

# Wait a moment
time.sleep(10)

# Exit gracefully (This sequence is important.)
driver.close()            # shutdown the browser
driver.quit()             # close driver
sys.exit()                # exit from the program
```

Script 4.4, The full script for Chapter 4

## CHAPTER 5

PROJ 02: INTRODUCING A FRAMEWORK

Now that we've tested our environment, let's create a framework to build robust bots.

This framework provides a place for our bots to exist. Primarily, the framework relieves the developer from a lot of busy-work and provides order through standardization. Standardization may sound like a crimp on a developer's creativity. But nothing can be further from the truth. A good framework can speed development by not having to reinvent yourself every time you want to load Webdriver or log an event.

This project introduces a framework that predefines project paths, does general configuration, and provides access to logging, file, parsing, and general bot libraries.

Watch the associated video on YouTube

There is a supplemental video on YouTube where you can watch demonstration of this bot as well as a narrated code walk-through. Go to www.mepso.com and click on the link for this book on the home page. You'll find links to videos and library code downloads there.

Figure 5.1, Link to supplemental video

Creating a framework

As one's career progresses—and more bots are written, developers tend to reuse those aspects of prior projects that worked particularly well. Over time, libraries and procedures become institutionalized into something that is used to speed development and help ensure reliability and maintainability of every bot project going forward. That's a healthy way to view this framework.

Calling `framework.py` a "framework" might be a bit of a stretch, because it shares a lot of those minimal characteristics of the prior chapter. But it also facilitates essential concepts that make projects easier to maintain, quicker to develop, and more tolerant to faults.

Though it's not a lot of code, this framework provides a lot of functionality in a small, stable, codebase. For example, one important thing that must be done every time you fire-up a bot is describe the paths for the libraries you use. At the very least, you'll have to tell your bot where to find the Webdriver. The framework then uses those paths to—not only load Webdriver, but also load standard Python libraries, and also custom bot-related libraries that speed and formalize development. Part of those libraries are used to provide a timestamped logging system that writes both to the console, but a log file as well. This log file is particularly useful when you have to debug a bot that has already run, perhaps hours or days earlier. In addition to the logging, the framework facilitates—even encourages, the developer to create a bot that exhibits human traits. Finally the framework cleanly closes.

Framework v. helloWorld

It might be useful—as a way to explaining this framework, to compare it to the bot we just played with in Chapter 4. More precisely lets compare their outputs.

While the helloWord example loaded a web page, it also wrote a few lines to the console, as shown below.

```
%> python helloWorld.py
DevTools listening on ws://127.0.0.1:55629/devtools/browser/08aef34f-3fc6-4fac-a427-
55ba79121f57
%>
```

Script 5.1 Output of helloWorld.py

On the console, the only sign that the helloWorld program ran is the Webdriver announcement, which is echoed automatically when Webdriver is loaded. If you were to see the console message without context, it wouldn't describe much about what happened. There is nothing that could assisting a developer in debugging problems that may have happened. For that matter, the information written to the console by helloWorld don't even indicate what time the program was run.

52

In contrast, `framework.py` writes a fair amount of useful information to the console, as shown in Figure 5.2.

```
2023-06-02 15:30:43: ##########################################
2023-06-02 15:30:43: # framework.py
2023-06-02 15:30:43: ##########################################
2023-06-02 15:30:43: Log file: LOG_20230602_153043.log
2023-06-02 15:30:43: Loading Chromedriver

DevTools listening on ws://127.0.0.1:55750/devtools/browser/56608221-1251-455f-83c5-
b3e496f52641
2023-06-02 15:30:45: Setting window size to 800px by 400px.
2023-06-02 15:30:45: Positioning window to 100, 100.
2023-06-02 15:30:45: Do something useful, load a website...
2023-06-02 15:30:46: Waiting 12
2023-06-02 15:30:46: 12, 11, 10, 9, 8, 7, 6, 5, 4, 3, 2, 1,
2023-06-02 15:30:57: Shutting down program: framework.py
2023-06-02 15:30:59: Execution time: 16.56 seconds.
```

Script 5.2, Output of template.py

The console output, shown above in Script 5.2, shows the advantages to formalized logging, including each of the following points:

1. **Auto Log Management** The framework automatically deletes old log files, and creates a new one, which it describes in the log. This code could be modified to save all logs, or to rotate them on a regular basis. These logs have infinite value, especially when you're trying to debug a bot that failed a few hours ago. Your log should provide a complete explanation of what happened and where the failure occurred.

2. **Time Stamping** Everything that is written to the log is timestamped. This not only allows the developer to know when events happened, but it also provides information as to how long it took to complete a section of the Python script.

3. **Auto Logging** Many of the functions in the framework automatically log their actions. You can tell which functions these are because the first parameter passed to them is a reference to the log file.

4. **Random Delays** In an attempt to look "less like a computer", the framework provides a randomWait() function, where the function waits a random amount of time determined by a minimum and maximum number of seconds you want the bot to wait. As the time expires, the console will tic the seconds away, so you're not left in a lurch, wondering how much longer the bot intends to wait. This is a simple way to ensure that your bot doesn't repeatedly leave the exact same set of log files in the web server it accesses.

Interfacing to the framework

A goal was to keep the framework as simple as possible. To that extent, it's been abstracted into very basic parts:

- The preamble (where things are configured),
- The payload (where your code goes), and
- The closing (where the program closes gracefully), as shown below.

```
######################################################
# FRAMEWORK FORMAT:
######################################################


######################################################
PREAMBLE:
        1. Defines script name,
        2. Defines paths
        3. Imports framework functions
#--------------------------


######################################################
PAYLOAD:
        Your bot code goes here...!
#--------------------------


######################################################
CLOSING:
        1. Close the browser
        2. Close selenium
        3. Exit Python
#--------------------------
```

Script 5.3, Framework workflow

What you see is a framework that is a compromise between simplicity and functionality. In another environment, an argument could be made to import each of these framework parts as libraries, opposed to the cut-and-paste method the book uses. But again…, simplicity.

Preamble, part 1

The first thing the framework does in the preamble is define the name of the script. The name of he script is defined early so it is available for the written log file.

Following that, the framework loads the python system libraries that are used in every bot.

```
########################################################################
scriptName = "framework" + " " + "rev0.1"
#---------------------------

# # # # # # # # # # # # # # #
# Configuration
import   sys
import   os
import   time

from     datetime import datetime
from     random   import   randint

import   selenium
from     selenium.Webdriver.common.by import By
from     selenium.Webdriver.common.keys import Keys

# Set the implicit wait time to 120 seconds (adjust as needed)
wait_time = 120
driver.implicitly_wait(wait_time)
```

Script 5.4, Part 1, preamble of the framework

Following the script name definition, the preamble of the framework imports the
community supplied libraries we use. This list includes:

sys   which allows us to perform system (IO) functions,

os   provides access to the operating system,

time   is a library of time and calendar functions,

datetime   provides additional time and date formatting

randint   is need for random number generation,

selenium   is the interface to Webdriver and the browser, and

liburl   this library is used in the CAPTCHA solving project.

It's important to note that the libraries imported here may not be a complete set of all
system libraries used by this book. There are also useful Python libraries for using
databases, spreadsheets, pdf files, and HTTP, that can be included as needed. The reason
for not including them every time is that they also consume resources. And if code isn't
needed, it's best not to load it.

The last act of the first part of the preamble is to set the default amount of time selenium
will wait for a web page to download. In this case, selenium will wait up to two minutes

for a page load to complete. If it takes longer than that to download the page, the program will time-out and terminate.

Preamble, part 2

The second part of the preamble defines when the script was started, and establishes all the project paths. This is a very useful part of the framework, because not only does it releave you from having to figure this out every time, it also keeps your file system neater because all bots are treated the same way. The second half of the preamble is shown below.

```
# # # # # # # # # # # # # #
# Record the start time
start_time = time.time()
timeStart = datetime.today().strftime('%Y%m%d_%H%M%S')

# # # # # # # # # # # # # # #
# Establish paths and import libraries
#
sys.path.insert(0, "../../libs")          # Import local libraries
from libPaths          import logFile
from libPaths          import pathChromeDriver

import libBot          # Useful bot functions
import libParse        # Parse functions
import libSelenium     # Selenium (Chromedriver) specific functions
```

Script 5.5, Part 2, framework preamble

Once the paths are established, they are used to load the book's custom libraries. These resources are:

libBot

A library containing operational functions, including those that control: logging, file IO, and randomness. This library is the core of the framework.

libParse

This is a library of parsing routines that were originally written in PHP and used in my first two books. So, they should look familiar if you're joining us from that direction. Here, the library has been rewritten in Python and slightly refined. These parsing functions are used throughout this book's examples. Additionally, Chapter 18, "Parsing and the semantic web", is dedicated to exchanging +25 years of parsing experience with specific instructions hon how to use this library.

libSelenium

This final library contains functions related to Selenium. These functions include loading Webdriver, setting browser location, and setting the browser screen window size. While `lib.Selenium.loadWebdriver()` facilitates loading Webdriver, this library also avails `lib.Selenium.loadHeadlessWebdriver()`. The entirety of Project 10, "Headless browsing" is dedicated to using this function.

Preamble, part 3

This third, and final, section of the preamble manages logs by deleting any old ones and starting a new one. You could modify this to cycle, retain, or even email, logs as well at your option. This is also the first used of libBot, where it is used to create the log file.

```
##############################
# Manage Logs
try:
    os.system("del *.log")
except:
    libBot.writeLog(logFile, "There were no log files to remove.")

##############################
# Establish log title
print()
libBot.writeLog(logFile, "#############################################")
libBot.writeLog(logFile, "# " + scriptName)
libBot.writeLog(logFile, "#############################################")
libBot.writeLog(logFile, "Log file: " + logFile)

##############################
# Load Selenium (get driver) and resize/reposition the browser window
try:
    driver = libSelenium.loadWebdriver(logFile, pathChromeDriver)
    libSelenium.setWindowSize(logFile, driver, x=800, y=400)
    libSelenium.setWindowPosition(logFile, driver, x=100, y=100)
except:
    libBot.writeLog(logFile, "Could not load Webdriver.")
```

Script 5.6, Framework preamble part 3

Once the log file is established, the name of the script is written to the log. This is followed by loading Selenium, which in this case is not the headless version, so the browser may also be sized and positioned.

As mentioned in the first section, I typically host bots in AWS and use remote access tools to work on them. I've learned that when your development platform has a large display—like my 43" 4K monitor, it's important to position your bots near the upper left corner of the monitor, or you will not be able to view them when you access your bot via a laptop, phone, or tablet with a smaller screen geometry.

The payload

The payload is simply where you put your specific bot script. Scripts in the payload area can operate independently while having access to all the tools in the framework.

```
#########################################################################
#########################################################################
## Start: PAYLOAD
##

# Get web page
libBot.writeLog(logFile, "Fetch a web page")
driver.get("https://www.mepso.com/helloWorld.html")
libBot.randomWait(logFile, 2, 3)

# Write web page to hTML file
libBot.writeLog(logFile, "Write web page to a file")
html = libBot.getWebpageContents(logFile, driver)        # get copy of html content
libBot.writeFile(logFile, "PageContents.html", html)     # write to file

##
## Endof: PAYLOAD
#########################################################################
#########################################################################
```

Script 5.7, A Simple framework payload

The payload in the script above features a few more framework functions. Here we can see libBot employed to:

1. Write logs,
2. Load web pages into the browser,
3. Facilitate random delays, and

59

4. to grab and save screen content.

The advantage here is that everything the bot needed had already been set-up in the preamble. And everything that's needed after is described next in the closure.

Framework closure

Just as it's important to initiate your bot according to procedure, it's also important to shut your bot down in a specific order. That sequence is defined in the script below.

```
##############################
# Close gracefully
libBot.writeLog(logFile, "Shutting down program: "+scriptName)

driver.close()   # close browser
driver.quit()    # close Webdriver

programDuration = time.time() - start_time
libBot.writeLog(logFile, "Execution time: " + f"{programDuration:,.2f}" + " seconds.")

sys.exit()
```
Script 5.8, A formalized exit to our bot scripts

The shutdown sequence works like this. The first thing that closed is the browser window. After the browser is closed, the active instance of Webdriver is shut down. Just before the Python program is ended, the runtime length is documented.

Chapter wrap

This chapter discusses the creation of a framework for building robust bots. The framework aims to enhance development efficiency and maintainability while incorporating essential features. It emphasizes the importance of standardization and the separation of active code from the framework. The framework's key components include loading libraries, implementing random delays, separating active code, and logging events.

The framework is intended to be a compromise between simplicity and functionality. It consists of several parts:

- **The preamble** defines the script's name and revision level, imports necessary system and custom libraries, and establishes project paths. It also manages log files, creates a new log, and loads Selenium (browser automation tool).

- **The payload** is where specific bot code is placed. It can use the libraries and configuration established in the preamble.

- **The exit** gracefully shuts down the program. It closes the browser, terminates the Webdriver instance, records the execution time, and exits the Python script.

This simple framework provides benefits such as formalized logging, timestamped events, automatic log creation and management, random delays, and more. It's designed to help developers create bots efficiently, maintain code consistency, and enhance debugging capabilities.

Don't forget to view the accompanying video, whose link appears at the beginning of this chapter.

Log: output

The following is an example log output for this bot.

```
2023-06-06 10:14:28: ###########################################
2023-06-06 10:14:28: # framework.py rev01
2023-06-06 10:14:28: ###########################################
2023-06-06 10:14:28: Log file: LOG_20230606_101428.log
2023-06-06 10:14:28: Loading Chromedriver
DevTools listening on ws://127.0.0.1:51534/devtools/browser/48a032df-7e71-4e35-930c-
9b3fdf9f7f79
2023-06-06 10:14:30: Setting window size to 800px by 400px.
2023-06-06 10:14:30: Positioning window to 100, 100.
2023-06-06 10:14:30: Fetch a web page
2023-06-06 10:14:32: Waiting 3
2023-06-06 10:14:32: 3, 2, 1,
2023-06-06 10:14:34: Write web page to a file
2023-06-06 10:14:34: Capturing screen contents
2023-06-06 10:14:34: Writing file: PageContents.html
2023-06-06 10:14:34: Shutting down program: framework.py
2023-06-06 10:14:37: Execution time: 8.89 seconds.
```

Script 5.7, Output, written to both the lof file and the console.

The little snippet above can be very valuable for documenting what your bot did. It's also invaluable to debugging errors that occurred when you wheren't around.

Script: Framework

```
####################################################################
scriptName = "framework" + ".py"
#--------------------------

# # # # # # # # # # # # # #
# Configuration
import   sys
import   os
import   time

from     datetime import datetime
from     random   import   randint

import   selenium
from      selenium.webdriver.common.by import By
from      selenium.webdriver.common.keys import Keys

# # # # # # # # # # # # # #
# Record the start time
start_time = time.time()
timeStart = datetime.today().strftime('%Y%m%d_%H%M%S')

# # # # # # # # # # # # # #
# Establish paths and import libraries
#
try:
        sys.path.insert(0, "../../libs")          # Import local libraries
        from libPaths          import logFile
        from libPaths          import pathChromeDriver
except:
        print("Unable to load one or more of the project paths")
        sys.exit()

try:
        import libBot           # Useful bot functions

        import libParse         # Parse functions

        import libSelenium       # Selenium (chromedriver) specific functions

except:
        print("Unable to load one or more of the project libraries")
        sys.exit()

# # # # # # # # # # # # # #
# Manage Logs
try:
        os.system("del *.log")
except:
        libBot.writeLog(logFile, "There were no log files to remove.")
```

```
libBot.writeLog(logFile, "\n")
libBot.writeLog(logFile, "###########################################")
libBot.writeLog(logFile, "# " + scriptName)
libBot.writeLog(logFile, "###########################################")
libBot.writeLog(logFile, "Log file: " + logFile)

# Load Selenium (get driver) and resize/reposition the browser window
try:
        driver = libSelenium.loadWebdriver(logFile, pathChromeDriver)
        libSelenium.setWindowSize(logFile, driver, x=1100, y=1100)
        libSelenium.setWindowPosition(logFile, driver, x=100, y=100)
except:
        print("Unable to load Webdriver")
        sys.exit()

###########################################################################
###########################################################################
## Start: PAYLOAD (This is where the work is preformed.)
##

# Get web page
libBot.writeLog(logFile, "Fetch a web page")
try:
        driver.get("https://www.mepso.com/helloWorld")
        libBot.randomWait(logFile, 4, 5)
except:
        libBot.closeBot(logFile, driver, "Unable to load Webdriver")

# Write web page to HTML file
libBot.writeLog(logFile, "Write web page to a file")
html = libBot.getWebpageContents(logFile, driver)
libBot.writeFile(logFile, "PageContents.html", html)

libBot.writeLog(logFile, "Capture a screen shot")
try:
        driver.save_screenshot("screenshot.png")
except:
        libBot.closeBot(logFile, driver, "Unable to save screenshot")


# ENDOF Payload
###########################################################################
###########################################################################

# # # # # # # # # # # # # # #
# Close gracefully
libBot.closeBot(logFile, driver, "Exiting normally: "+scriptName)
###########################################################################
```

## CHAPTER 6

PROJ 03: AJAX AND ACTIVE CONTENT

When AJAX *(Asynchronous JavaScript and XML)* was introduced, it brought significant changes in the way web applications were built and interact with visitors. Prior to AJAX, web pages followed a traditional client-server model, where client requests were made once, to which one HTML file was recieved from the server. AJAX revolutionized web development by facilitating *Active Content,* or Asynchronous Page Loading between the client and the server—without the need for page reflows.

This chapter introduces the following topics:

- The effect that AJAX had on the botDev community,
- Background on XMLHttpRequest, and how it's used, and
- How to effectively manage with asynchronous page loading.

Watch the associated video on YouTube

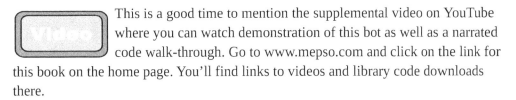

This is a good time to mention the supplemental video on YouTube where you can watch demonstration of this bot as well as a narrated code walk-through. Go to www.mepso.com and click on the link for this book on the home page. You'll find links to videos and library code downloads there.

Figure 6.1, Supplemental chapter video

A little background

The web broke the client-server model in 1999 when Microsoft introduced an XMLHttpRequest object as an Active X control for Internet Explorer 5. Though it preceded Netscape's XMLHttpRequest, it was designed to do what AJAX eventually did—simply, to allow additional communication between the browser and web server after the web page was initially loaded. Active content wasn't commonly found on the

Internet until quite a while after it was available. But as developers recognized the potential of using XMLHttpRequest for building more interactive and dynamic web applications, other browsers started implementing unified support for it.

> You can read more about the `XMLHttpRequest` object in *Chapter 15, "DOM, and JavaScript"*.

Developers were slow to adopt the new asynchronous page loading techniques. Their hesitation stemmed from several factors. Firstly, inconsistency arose due to differing approaches taken by Netscape and Microsoft. Microsoft's use of the Windows-only ActiveX control further complicated matters, alienating Mac and Unix users. Moreover, concerns about the security implications of tightly integrating ActiveX controls with the Windows Operating System deterred many developers and web users. Consequently, initial developer support for asynchronous page loading was severely limited.

Adding to these issues, a lack of comprehensive documentation hindered the implementation of AJAX-powered applications. This absence of guidance was unfortunate, considering that the process itself is not overly complex.

AJAX wasn't standardized by the *W3C*, or World Wide Web Consortium, until 2006. Prior to that, AJAX didn't get much play. The one exception may be *gMail*, Google's email application, which used active content in 2005. But it also required the use of the Chrome browser, which sped its adaptation.

Challenges AJAX poses to web developers

While AJAX created new opportunities for developers to create immersive online experiences, it also became a real pain to those of us, who develop bots. Up until AJAX, any web page—regardless of complexity, could be downloaded with very simple software, It was so easy that web pages can be downloaded with a simple Telnet client.

But these enhanced user experience came at the cost of complexity. And a side effect that complexity meant that bot developers could no longer rely on the first page download to ensure access to the entire web page. Any additional button clicks that downloaded fresh data to a table or any endless page scroll meant that bot developers would not access any of the subsequent data downloads. This presented major questions for bot developers.

Fortunately, Selenium has answers. And AJAX no longer poses problems for bot developers.

Our target page

The target web page is very simple, but it focuses on the creation of active content. On first download, the page is bare, with the exception of a button labeled "Load Data".

Figure *6*.2, The *target* web page, *as it looks before the button press*

If you look at the source code for that page, you see the following:

```
<!DOCTYPE html>
<html>
<body>
<button id="btn1" type="button" onClick="loadData()">Load Data</button>

<div id="data"></div>

<script src="script.js"></script>

</body>
</html>
```

Script 6.1, The target page source code

The target page essentially has a button that calls a JavaScript function called `loadData()` and the inclusion of the JavaScript file, script.js, that holds that function.

67

A copy of the JavaScript file is shown below.

```
function loadData() {
    var xhr = new XMLHttpRequest();

    xhr.open("GET", "http://www.mepso.com/selenium_python/examples/async/file.txt", true);

    xhr.onreadystatechange = function () {
        if (xhr.readyState == 4 && xhr.status == 200) {
            document.getElementById("data").innerHTML = xhr.responseText;
        }
    }
    xhr.send();
}
```

Script 6.2, The JavaScript that dynamically downloads the additional data.

The JavaScript code above is activated when the button (labeled "Load Data") is pressed. The `loadData()` function accesses a remote file named `file.txt` and loads it into a `<DIV>` created by the calling HTML file.

An example of what the target page looks like once the button is pressed is shown below.

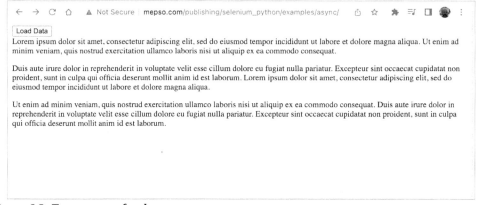

Figure 6.2, Target page after button press

Capturing the content of this webpage would have been very difficult before Selenium. With Selenium it's pretty easy, as you'll see.

Code walk-through

This is the first of the examples to use the template defined in the last chapter. Since we are using the template, we will limit our discussion to that of the payload, where this bot code will go.

The code is simple. The first action of the payload is to download the target web page with the active content, as shown in the script below.

```
######################################################################
######################################################################
## Start: PAYLOAD (This is where the work is performed.)
##

# Get web page
url = "http://www.mepso.com/publishing/selenium_python/examples/async/"
libBot.writeLog(logFile, "Getting: " + url)
driver.get(url)
libBot.randomWait(logFile, 2, 3)

# Trigger the event
libBot.writeLog(logFile, "Press the button")
driver.find_element(By.ID, "btn1").click()
libBot.randomWait(logFile, 2, 3)

# Capture and log the active content
dataDiv = driver.find_element(By.ID, "data")
activeContent = dataDiv.get_attribute('innerHTML')
libBot.writeLog(logFile, "The active content is: "+ activeContent)
libBot.randomWait(logFile, 2, 3)

# ENDOF Payload
######################################################################
######################################################################
```

Script 6.3, Payload of the asyncBot

Once the target page is downloaded, we trigger the event by using the click() function of the selenium find_element() object. This is the first time we're using Selenium to interact with a web element, so let's give this some soace.

How Selenium finds things

Like JavaScript, Selenium primarily finds web objects via the DOM, or Document Object Model. The first time this is done, in the script above, is when Python executes the `driver.find_element(By.ID, "")` function. If you are at all familiar with

JavaScript, you should notice the similarity with JavaScript's `document.findElementByID()` function. Both the JavaScript and the Selenium commands do the same thing, return an identifier object for the DOM element requested. By adding the `.click()`, Selenium "clicks" on the object.

Selenium timeouts

The bot then waits a random period of two to three seconds. After that period, it is assumed that the active content is downloaded.

*Selenium will wait for a web page to load. It's important to remember, however, that Selenium will only wait for **initial** page flows. Information obtained from the server after the page has been initially flowed works outside of the regular client-server process. So those transactions are not included in the default page timeout period. In other words, if your bot requests active content, it will either have to wait a prescribed period and hope the data has arrived. Or it must somehow detect that the data has been received.*

```
# Set the implicit wait time to 120 seconds (adjust as needed)
wait_time = 120
driver.implicitly_wait(wait_time)
```
Script 6.4, Setting default page download period

Capturing the new content is relatively straightforward. The DIV, where the new text goes, it located with the `find_element` object. Once identified, a variable named, "activeContent" is loaded with the innerHTML of the DIV found earlier. That data is then displayed to the log, as proof that it was collected.

Here is the log file for the entire operation.

```
2023-06-17 15:33:15: ##############################################
2023-06-17 15:33:15: # activeContent.py
2023-06-17 15:33:15: ##############################################
2023-06-17 15:33:15: Log file: LOG_20230617_153315.log
2023-06-17 15:33:15: Loading chromedriver
Incompatible release of chromedriver (version 113.0.5672.63) detected in PATH: C:\Users\
Administrator\Desktop\bots\selenium_python\libs\Webdrivers\chromedriver.exe

DevTools listening on ws://127.0.0.1:59478/devtools/browser/a79091d1-80dc-43ec-bf7e-
754e76ab3c7c
2023-06-17 15:33:21: Setting window size to 800px by 800px.
2023-06-17 15:33:21: Positioning window to 10, 10.
2023-06-17 15:33:21: Getting:
http://www.mepso.com/publishing/selenium_python/examples/async/
2023-06-17 15:33:21: Waiting 2
2023-06-17 15:33:21: 2, 1,
2023-06-17 15:33:22: Press the button
2023-06-17 15:33:22: Waiting 3
2023-06-17 15:33:22: 3, 2, 1,
2023-06-17 15:33:24: The active content is: Lorem ipsum dolor sit amet, consectetur
adipiscing elit, sed do eiusmod tempor incididunt ut labore et dolore magna aliqua. Ut enim
ad minim veniam, quis nostrud exercitation ullamco laboris nisi ut aliquip ex ea commodo
consequat.
<p>
Duis aute irure dolor in reprehenderit in voluptate velit esse cillum dolore eu fugiat
nulla pariatur. Excepteur sint occaecat cupidatat non proident, sunt in culpa qui officia
deserunt mollit anim id est laborum.
Lorem ipsum dolor sit amet, consectetur adipiscing elit, sed do eiusmod tempor incididunt
ut labore et dolore magna aliqua.
</p><p>
Ut enim ad minim veniam, quis nostrud exercitation ullamco laboris nisi ut aliquip ex ea
commodo consequat. Duis aute irure dolor in reprehenderit in voluptate velit esse cillum
dolore eu fugiat nulla pariatur. Excepteur sint occaecat cupidatat non proident, sunt in
culpa qui officia deserunt mollit anim id est laborum.
</p>
2023-06-17 15:33:24: Waiting 2
2023-06-17 15:33:24: 2, 1,
2023-06-17 15:33:25: Shutting down program: async.py
2023-06-17 15:33:30: Execution time: 15.55 seconds.
```

Script 6.5, The resulting log generated by the bot.

The full script is depicted on the successive pages.

Script

```
####################################################################
scriptName = "activeContent" + ".py"
#---------------------------

# # # # # # # # # # # # # #
# Configuration
import   sys
import   os
import   time

from     datetime        import datetime
from     random          import randint
s
import   selenium
from     selenium.webdriver.common.by import By
from     selenium.webdriver.common.keys import Keys

# # # # # # # # # # # # # #
# Record the start time
start_time = time.time()
timeStart = datetime.today().strftime('%Y%m%d_%H%M%S')

# # # # # # # # # # # # # # #
# Establish paths and import libraries
#
sys.path.insert(0, "../../libs")          # Import local libraries
from libPaths          import logFile
from libPaths          import pathChromeDriver
from libPaths          import pathRoot

import libBot          # Useful bot functions

import libParse        # Parse functions

import libSelenium      # Selenium (chromedriver) specific functions


# # # # # # # # # # # # # # #
# Manage Logs
try:
        os.system("del *.log")
except:
        libBot.writeLog(logFile, "There were no log files to remove.")

print("\n")
libBot.writeLog(logFile, "#############################################")
libBot.writeLog(logFile, "# " + scriptName)
libBot.writeLog(logFile, "#############################################")
libBot.writeLog(logFile, "Log file: " + logFile)

# Load Selenium (get driver) and resize/reposition the browser window
```

72

```
driver = libSelenium.loadWebdriver(logFile, pathChromeDriver)
libSelenium.setWindowSize(logFile, driver, x=800, y=800)
libSelenium.setWindowPosition(logFile, driver, x=10, y=10)

########################################################################
########################################################################
## Start: PAYLOAD (This is where the work is performed.)
##

# Get web page
url = "http://www.mepso.com/publishing/selenium_python/examples/activeContent/"
libBot.writeLog(logFile, "Getting: " + url)
driver.get(url)
libBot.randomWait(logFile, 5, 7)

# Trigger the event
libBot.writeLog(logFile, "Press the button")
driver.find_element(By.ID, "btn1").click()
libBot.randomWait(logFile, 5, 7)

# Capture and log the active content
dataDiv = driver.find_element(By.ID, "data")
activeContent = dataDiv.get_attribute('innerHTML')
libBot.writeLog(logFile, "The active content is: "+ activeContent)
libBot.randomWait(logFile, 2, 3)



# ENDOF Payload
########################################################################
########################################################################

# # # # # # # # # # # # # # #
# Close gracefully
libBot.closeBot(logFile, driver, "Exiting normally: "+scriptName)
########################################################################
```

Script 6.6, Complete script for active content example

One of the more common bot tasks is that of ordering products, or evaluating available inventory levels. This bot shows how to:

1. Size-up the website and see what your bot needs to accomplish,

2. Authenticate into a website,

3. Order products, and

4. Obtain a receipt.

Like the other projects, this *procurementBot* is designed to work with a special website designed specifically for you to practice on. This relieves you from having to practice on a real commerce website. So, you will be able to practice without actually spending money or making mistakes on a real retail website. We'll be using an online store that sells cups—created specifically for this project.

These types of procurement projects offer many opportunities for further automation and are often combined with other bots that either watch inventory or market prices.

Watch the associated video on YouTube

There is an associated video on YouTube where you can watch demonstration of this bot as well as a narrated code walk-through. Go to www.mepso.com and click on the link for this book on the home page. You'll also find links to videos and library code downloads there.

Figure 7.1, Link to chapter video

If you have questions regarding this project, please check the comment area at the project's video. If I can't answer your question, someone else probably can.

Surveying the website

Before you start writing any bot, it's important to learn as much as possible from the website your bot will target. The better you understand how a web site works, the better you will be able to write that specific bot. Here's a quick look at this project's target.

For our purposes, we'll (pretend that we will) be buying product from the Boynton Plastic Cup Factory Outlet. We have good terms with this company and they allow purchases with only a purchase order number.

Figure 7.2, Authentication page at target

It should be noted that there was no real attempt to build security into this test website. That wasn't the point. So please don't try to hack into this store. It's not that hard and it's no prize.

Once authenticated, the website will take you directly to the order form. When you get here the order form will be blank. The form shown in Figure has the specified order details already entered.

Figure 7.3, The order form, with products selected

The interface in Figure 7.3 is a good one for our purposes because it showcases selenium's ability to control a variety of web form controls.

76

Once the "Order Now" button is pressed, the order is placed, and a record of the order is displayed.

Figure 7.4, A receipt completed order

Our procurementBot will save a copy of the receipt, shown in Figure 7.4, in a file and then exit.

Code walk-through

This script is a little more complicated than earlier bots because we have to complete a sequence of events, including: Authentication, Placing an order, and Saving a receipt.

In software development, it's a generally accepted rule that Research and Development should be separate activities. In other words, the software should be designed before it is coded. This is also the ideal with bot development, but it can be complicated because browser interactions are less predictable and can change with use.

The Framework

We'll again be using the framework defined in Project 2. As you recall, the framework is primarily a preamble that initializes the bot's environment. We'll insert the actual bot code for this project after the preamble in the payload section. Once the bot code completes, it will fall into the framework's exit and close gracefully.

Initializations

In the payload section of the program, we need to initialize some application related variables that are not made in the framework. Remember again, that all of this code is placed in what was the payload section of the framework.

```
######################################################################
######################################################################
## Start: PAYLOAD (This is where the work is performed.)
##

# App initialization
username = "Selenium"
password = "Python"
loginPath = "http://www.mepso.com/publishing/selenium_python/"
loginPage = loginPath + "examples/cupOrder/"
PONumber = "123ABC"
```

Script 7.1, Payload initializations

Security concerns

In Script 7.1, we make define some application-level variables, mostly for authentication. You'll notice that both the username and password for the target website are in cleartext, so anyone, who can view the code, can also see the login credentials. This is a common problem; one which database administrators are all too familiar.

Perhaps the best way to solve the problem of passwords in cleartext is to place the credentials in a file that is not in webspace and in a directory only accessible to the bot. Encrypting or obfuscating passwords usually means that there also needs to be a method to decrypt and elucidate. I've toyed with password servers too, but think that securing in the file structure is probably the best approach to securing application passwords..

Authentication

The code snippet in Script 7.2 shows how the bot manages the authentication form. In general, completing authentication is no different than submitting any other HTML form.

```
######################################################################
# STARTOF: Authentication
# Get initial webpage
libBot.writeLog(logFile, "Get initial webpage")
try:
    driver.get(loginPage)
    libBot.randomWait(logFile, 3, 5)
except:
    libBot.writeLog(logFile, loginPage + " could not be loaded.")

# Enter username
libBot.writeLog(logFile, "Entering username: " + username)
try:
    driver.find_element(By.NAME, "username").click()
    libBot.randomWait(logFile, 2, 3)
    driver.find_element(By.NAME, "username").send_keys(username)
    libBot.randomWait(logFile, 2, 3)
except:
    libBot.writeLog(logFile, "Username field could not be found.")

# enter password
libBot.writeLog(logFile, "Entering password: ########")
try:
    driver.find_element(By.NAME, "password").click()
    libBot.randomWait(logFile, 2, 3)
    driver.find_element(By.NAME, "password").send_keys(password)
    libBot.randomWait(logFile, 2, 3)
except:
    libBot.writeLog(logFile, "Username field could not be found.")

# Submit credentials
libBot.writeLog(logFile, "Submitting credentials")
try:
    driver.find_element(By.ID, "loginButton").click()
except:
    libBot.writeLog(logFile, "Submit button could not be found.")
# ENDOF: Authentication
```

Script 7.2, Managing authentication

If you were to view the source of the web page—or if you used *Chrome Inspect*, (as described in Chapter 23) you'd see that the user name and password fields, in the target website, were identified with NAME attributes of "username" and "password". These are the identifiers we'll use to assist Selenium in locating these web elements.

Again, Selenium uses location techniques that mirror those found in JavaScript. For example, to find the Password form element, Selenium uses the Selenium Python function,

```
webObject = driver.find_element(By.NAME, "object name").
```

Something very similar is done later with the password field.

Later, in this same script, we identify the LoginButton by it's ID with a Selenium Python line that loos like:

```
webObject = driver.find_element(By.ID, "object id").
```

 I like to click on a field before I enter any data into that field. I'm bringing this up now because the inclination for inexperienced bot developers is to locate the field and immediately insert the data— something not humanly possible. Instead, I prefer to click on the text-box first, as a person would, wait a short random period of time, and then enter the data. Again, the reason I take—what look like evasive measures, is because it's wise to look at your bot as a trade secret, and handle it appropriately.

The bot does essentially handles the username and password fields identically. The only difference are the identifiers and the data.

As you'll learn, there are several identifiers that can be used to identify web elements. This is a good thing, because, in the wild, you don't always have access to the same set of unique identifiers. So far, we've used ID and NAME.

The routine for submitting the username and password is similar to that of filling in those fields. But in this case, we use the submit button's ID instead of NAME.

Verifying landmarks

The term, Landmark, is usually used to identify important places on webpages. But, a landmark can also be used to indicate the very existence of a page.

After authentication, or any significant page transition, it's a good idea for a bot to verify that it is on the expected page. The way I usually do this is to capture a portion of the expected page, known as a Landmark and see if that landmark is found in the current page.

Figure 7.5, Validating landmarks.

In our case, we anticipate that the succeeding web page will have a landmark as described in the code below, in Script 7.3. The landmark value="Order Now" was chosen because the term "Order Now" becomes server data once the form is submitted. And I've learned that back-end software changes less often than the parts of web pages that control visual design and configuration.

```
# Verify landmark
html = libBot.getWebpageContents(logFile, driver)
landmark='value="Order Now"'

if libParse.stristr(html, landmark):
    libBot.writeLog(logFile, "Authenticated...!")
```

Script 7.3, Checking that landmarks are present

Selecting product (controlling form elements)

In the next code segment, Python uses Selenium to complete the form and submit our order. This form utilizes various form elements, including select lists, text boxes, checkboxes, radio controls, and buttons. Though this is a fairly diverse set of form elements, notice that Selenium controls these diverse elements in a similar manner, primarily with the find_element object.

```
################################################################
# STARTOF: Place cup order

# 12oz section
msg = "Placing order for 10 Dozen Clear 12oz Cups"
libBot.writeLog(logFile, msg)

# Select 12 oz Clear cups
driver.find_element(By.ID, "12ozColorClear").click()
libBot.randomWait(logFile, 2, 3)

# Select 10 Dozen 12oz cups
dropdown = driver.find_element(By.ID, "12ozDozQty")
optionXPATH="//option[. = '10 Dozen @ $7.00']"
```

```
dropdown.find_element(By.XPATH, optionXPATH).click()
```
Script 7.4, Selecting 12 oz cups

In order to select a 12oz cup, the bot will need to control a select list, or drop-down menu. That will require XPATH.

Introduction to XPATH

As alluded to earlier, there are several ways to identify web elements. So far, we've used NAME and ID attributes. This project introduces another widely used identifier called *XPATH*.

XPATH is particularly useful for identifying parts of web pages that are not form elements. We're only using a small part of XPATH in this project, but it's well worth reading Chapter 16, *"Selenium locators"*, where XPATH is explained in detail. But for now, know that XPATH is essentially a structured array that defines where page elements are located within the DOM or Document Object Model.

This array feature, while we're not using in this example, is extremely useful because the XPATH locator for a table cell is just an index increment away from the cell next to it, or the row below. This can make it easy to iterate though a table with XPATH and a for loop. We'll use this method in Project six.

XPATH is a powerful and flexible tool that can navigate through the hierarchical structure of an XML (or HTML) document and perform various operations, such as selecting nodes based on their attributes, finding specific elements or values, and traversing parent, child, or sibling relationships. XPATH is commonly used in web scraping and automation tools like Selenium, where it helps locate specific elements within the HTML (which can be treated as an XML document) of a web page. By using XPATH expressions, you can precisely target elements based on their attributes, position, or relationships with other elements, making it a valuable tool for tasks that involve complex navigation or manipulation of web page elements.

I tend to use NAME or ID as identifiers when they're available, but my next choice is nearly always XPATH, largely because I know it's always going to be available.

Finding a node's XPATH

There are other ways to determine the XPATH for web elements, but I prefer to use *Chrome Inspect.* The Chrome Inspect tool is described in detail in Chapter 23, *"Chrome Inspect"*. In fact, this is a good time to reference that chapter if you haven't.

For now, know that in Chrome, you can "right click" on any part of a web page and select "Inspect" from the resulting menu. This opens a tool on the right side of your chrome window. Now when you cursor over any web object on the page, your can "right mouse" and select "copy", where you will be rewarded with an option to copy the web element's XPATH. Again, this might be a good time to reference Chapter 23.

Controlling select lists

The reason we're discussing XPATH is because we need to use it to control the product select list, or drop-down list, that we saw back in Script 7.4. The process works like this:

- Selenium first exposes the "dropdown" object by clicking on the select list, in this case, found by using the NAME identifier.

- That dropdown object is then used to identify the desired option with an identifying method XPATH. That XPATH statement looks like this:

  ```
  optionXPATH="//option[. = '10 Dozen @ $7.00']".
  ```

For now, don't worry about how the XPATH was constructed. But in this case, it's obvious where the XPATH comes from, and after you've seen enough of these, they become obvious. Again, for a more sufficient explanation of how Chrome Inspect works, reference Chapters 23, *"Chrome Inspect"*. If you'd like to get a better understanding of XPATH, jump ahead to Chapter 16, *"Selenium Locators"*.

Selecting the 16 oz cups

After selecting 12 oz cups, the bot focuses on the 16 ounce cups, as shown in the succeeding script.

```
# 16oz section
msg = "Placing order for 100 Dozen Red 16oz Cups"
libBot.writeLog(logFile, msg)
```

```
# Select 16 oz Clear cups
driver.find_element(By.ID, "16ozColorRed").click()
libBot.randomWait(logFile, 2, 3)
# Select 100 Dozen 16oz cups
dropdown = driver.find_element(By.ID, "16ozDozQty")
optionXPATH = "//option[. = '100 Dozen @ $100.00']"
dropdown.find_element(By.XPATH, optionXPATH).click()
```

Script 7.5, Ordering 16 oz cups

The code in Script 7.5 above, is nearly identical to the way 12 oz cups were ordered. Only the quantities and form identifiers were changed to reflect the 16 oz merchandise.

Check boxes and radio controls

Most web objects are essentially controlled the same way. In most cases, one locates an object, using driver.find_element and then you click on that object, or enter a string.

It shouldn't surprise you that Selenium also uses familiar methods to control both checkboxes and radio controls.

```
# Select Tracking
driver.find_element(By.ID, "Tracking").click()
libBot.randomWait(logFile, 2, 3)
# Select Notifications
driver.find_element(By.ID, "Notify").click()
libBot.randomWait(logFile, 2, 3)
```

Script 7.6 Selecting delivery options (controlling check boxes)

Buttons

And it should come as no surprise that buttons are treated a lot like any other page element. But here we had the option of not clicking the button, but simply pressing the ENTER key in one of the form elements, which has the same effect as hitting a SUBMIT button.

```
# Submit order (no button id, just hit enter in PONumber field)
driver.find_element(By.NAME, "order-number").send_keys(PONumber)
libBot.randomWait(logFile, 2, 3)
driver.find_element(By.NAME, "order-number").send_keys(Keys.ENTER)
libBot.randomWait(logFile, 2, 3)
```

Script 7.7 Submitting the order (controlling buttons)

In this case, the bot effectively this the ENTER key instead of click on the SUBMIT button.

Saving a record of the purchase

Once the order is submitted, the webpage displays a recap of the order that was just placed. Here again, the bot uses Selenium's ability to execute Javascript to get the contents of the second table, which holds the record of the completed sale.

```
# Store a copy of the completed order
js = "return document.querySelector('table:nth-of-type(2)').innerHTML;"
orderPlaced = driver.execute_script(js)
orderFile = "ORDER_" + PONumber + ".html"
libBot.writeFile(logFile, orderFile, orderPlaced)
```
Script 7.8, Saving part of the web page to a file.

This information, in the string variable orderFile is then written to a file and referenced by its Purchase Order number.

Full script

```
######################################################################
scriptName = "cupOrder" + ".py"
#-------------------------

# # # # # # # # # # # # # #
# Configuration
import  sys
import  os
import  time

from    datetime import datetime
from    random  import  randint

import  selenium
from    elenium.webdriver.common.by import By
from    selenium.webdriver.common.keys import Keys

# # # # # # # # # # # # # #
# Record the start time
start_time = time.time()
timeStart = datetime.today().strftime('%Y%m%d_%H%M%S')

# # # # # # # # # # # # # #
# Establish paths and import libraries
#
sys.path.insert(0, "../../libs")        # Import local libraries
from libPaths           import logFile
from libPaths           import pathChromeDriver

import libBot           # Useful bot functions

import libParse         # Parse functions

import libSelenium      # Selenium (chromedriver) specific functions


# # # # # # # # # # # # # #
# Manage Logs
try:
        os.system("rm *.log")
except:
        libBot.writeLog(logFile, "There were no log files to remove.")

print("\n")
libBot.writeLog(logFile, "####################################")
libBot.writeLog(logFile, "# " + scriptName)
libBot.writeLog(logFile, "####################################")
libBot.writeLog(logFile, "Log file: " + logFile)

# Load Selenium (get driver) & resize/reposition the browser window
```

```
driver = libSelenium.loadWebdriver(logFile, pathChromeDriver)
libSelenium.setWindowSize(logFile, driver, x=1000, y=700)
libSelenium.setWindowPosition(logFile, driver, x=0, y=10)

#####################################################################
#####################################################################
## Start: PAYLOAD (This is where the work is preformed.)
##

# App initializations
username        = "Selenium"
password        = "Python"
loginPath       = "http://www.mepso.com/publishing/selenium_python/"
loginPage       = loginPath + "examples/cupOrder/"
PONumber        = "123ABC"

#####################################################################
# START OF: Authentication

# Get initial webpage
libBot.writeLog(logFile, "Get initial webpage")
driver.get(loginPage)
libBot.randomWait(logFile, 3, 5)

# Enter username
libBot.writeLog(logFile, "Entering username: " + username)
driver.find_element(By.NAME, "username").click()
libBot.randomWait(logFile, 2, 3)
driver.find_element(By.NAME, "username").send_keys(username)
libBot.randomWait(logFile, 2, 3)

# enter password
libBot.writeLog(logFile, "Entering password: ########")
driver.find_element(By.NAME, "password").click()
libBot.randomWait(logFile, 2, 3)
driver.find_element(By.NAME, "password").send_keys(password)
libBot.randomWait(logFile, 2, 3)

# Submit credentials
libBot.writeLog(logFile, "Submitting credentials")
driver.find_element(By.ID, "loginButton").click()

# END OF: Authentication
#####################################################################

# Verify landmark
html = libBot.getWebpageContents(logFile, driver)
landmark='value="Order Now"'

if libParse.stristr(html, landmark):
        libBot.writeLog(logFile, "Authenticated...!")
        libBot.randomWait(logFile, 2, 3)
```

```
################################################################
# START OF: Place cup order

# 12oz section
msg = "Placing order for 10 Dozen Clear 12oz Cups"
libBot.writeLog(logFile, msg)

# Select 12oz Clear cups
driver.find_element(By.ID, "12ozColorClear").click()
libBot.randomWait(logFile, 2, 3)

# Select 10 Dozen 12oz cups
dropdown = driver.find_element(By.ID, "12ozDozQty")
optionXPATH="//option[. = '10 Dozen @ $7.00']"
dropdown.find_element(By.XPATH, optionXPATH).click()

# Select 16oz Clear cups
msg = "Placing order for 100 Dozen Red 16oz Cups"
libBot.writeLog(logFile, msg)
driver.find_element(By.ID, "16ozColorRed").click()
libBot.randomWait(logFile, 2, 3)

# Select 100 Dozen 16oz cups
dropdown = driver.find_element(By.ID, "16ozDozQty")
optionXPATH = "//option[. = '100 Dozen @ $100.00']"
dropdown.find_element(By.XPATH, optionXPATH).click()

# Select Tracking
driver.find_element(By.ID, "Tracking").click()
libBot.randomWait(logFile, 2, 3)

# Select Rush Delivery
driver.find_element(By.ID, "Rush").click()
libBot.randomWait(logFile, 2, 3)

# Select Delivery Confirmation
driver.find_element(By.ID, "Notify").click()
libBot.randomWait(logFile, 2, 3)

# Submit order (no button id, just hit enter in PONumber field)
driver.find_element(By.NAME, "order-number").send_keys(PONumber)
libBot.randomWait(logFile, 2, 3)
driver.find_element(By.NAME, "order-number").send_keys(Keys.ENTER)
libBot.randomWait(logFile, 2, 3)

# Store a copy of the completed order
dataTable = driver.find_element(By.ID, "completedOrder")
orderTXT = dataTable.get_attribute('innerHTML')
orderFile = "ORDER_" + PONumber + ".html"
libBot.writeFile(logFile, orderFile, orderTXT)

libBot.randomWait(logFile, 10, 11)
```

```
else:
        libBot.closeBot(logFile, driver, "Unable to find auth landmark")

##
## ENDOF: PAYLOAD
##########################################################################
##########################################################################


# # # # # # # # # # # # # #
# Close gracefully
libBot.closeBot(logFile, driver, "Shutting down program: "+scriptName)
##########################################################################
```

Today's web developers are not restricted to yesterday's form elements. With advances to CSS and JavaScript, developers can now create immersive environments that often baffle bot developers.

That's because today's custom controls can use their own triggers, be affected by AJAX updates, use advanced CSS constructs, or employ such constructs as drag-and-drop.

Fortunately, these obstacles are no longer problems for bot developers that use Selenium.

Some of the highlights of this chapter include:

- The introduction of ActionChains; Selenium's way of managing complex user interaction—things like: drag-and-drop, right mouse clicks, etc., and
- How traditional techniques can sometimes be applied to custom form controls.

Watch the associated video on YouTube

There's a supplemental video on YouTube where you can watch a demonstration of this bot as well as a narrated code walk-through. Go to mepso.com and click on the link for this book on the home page. You'll also find links to videos and library code downloads there.

Figure 8.1, Link to chapter video

Examining the target

Like the other projects in this book. Our bot will be using a webpage that is specifically developed for this book. The target for this example bot project has a variety of non-standard controls and are from the JQuery libraries.

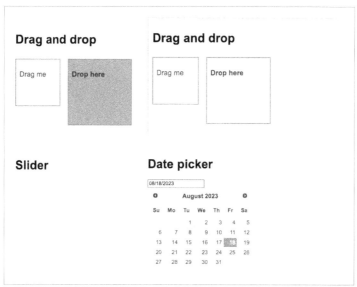

Figure 8.1, The target web page for custom control practice

The web page above contains four sets of controls. Going left to right, we have a drag-and-drop exercise, where the goal is to drag the small box onto the larger box.

This exercise is repeated to the right, but here the control is in an iframe. We will use this control to showcase a way to avoid a common bot-related drag-and-drop mistake.

In the lower left of the page, we see a simple JQuery slider control, whose traits are similar but yet distinct from a true drag-and-drop action. Finally, we have a JQuery calendar date picker.

This is certainly not an exhaustive list of what you might find in the wild—and new controls are developed all the time. But, these custom controls are quite representative of what you're apt to find. Understanding how to manipulate these controls will put you well on your way to figuring out how ActionChains work.

Code Walk-through

Let's take a look at the code. Like the others, this example also uses the framework developed in the second project.

This is one of the few projects that modifies the framework. This modification is done to accommodate ActionChains. The added code to import ActionChains is shown below in Script 8.1.

```
import   selenium
from     selenium.webdriver.common.by           import By
from     selenium.webdriver.common.keys          import Keys
from     selenium.webdriver.common.action_chains  import ActionChains
```

Script 8.1, Importing ActionChains

Again, back to the payload, the bot loads the target webpage, as shown below.

```
#####################################################################
#####################################################################
## Start: PAYLOAD (This is where the work is performed.)
##
print("Get page")
driver.get("http://mepso.com/exp/SP2_5.php")
driver.set_window_size(900, 875)
libBot.randomeWait(2, 3)
```

Script 8.2, Navigating to the example (target) web page.

In the few lines of script above, the program loads the target web page that contains the custom controls. After loading, it waits two or three seconds before proceeding. Technically this isn't required, but it's a good idea to delay before moving on because we want to simulate human behavior. And no one acts on a web page immediately after it's loaded.

Introducing ActionChains

ActionChains is a class in the Selenium Python library that provides ways to perform complex actions or sequences of actions on a web page. ActionChains allows you to automate complex mouse interactions, like: Right Click, Drag-and-Drop, Hover, and to make mouse movements.

93

With ActionChains, you can simulate user actions that go beyond simple single element interactions. It's called ActionChains because the ActionChains class provides methods to build a chain of actions, which are be executed either sequentially or as a composite action.

ActionChains methods

move_to_element()

> Moves the mouse cursor to the specified element on the page.

click()

> Performs a left mouse button click at the current mouse position.

context_click()

> Performs a right mouse button click at the current mouse position.

double_click()

> Performs a double left mouse button click at the current mouse position.

drag_and_drop(source, target)

> Drags an element from the source location and drops it onto the target location.

release()

> Essentially "unpresses" the active mouse button.

send_keys(keys)

> Sends keyboard keys to the active element on the page.

You'll notice that some of these methods are not unique to ActionChains. For example, `click()` and `send_keys()`. But the others, are new to ActionChains. By using these methods and chaining them together, you can create more complex interactions like mouse hovering, drag-and-drop operations, keyboard inputs, and more. Once you have defined your action sequence, you can perform the actions using the `perform()` method of the ActionChains object.

Overall, ActionChains provides a flexible and powerful way to automate user interactions with web pages using Selenium in Python, as we'll see.

In the first drag and drop, we simply use ActionChains with the drag_and_drop() method. The code is really simple. The bot only needs to define the object to be dragged, and the object to drag it to. To make the chain of actions execute, we add perform() to the end of the chain of events.

Conducting our first drag-and-drop operation

The first step in conducting a drag-and-drop action is to identify the web elements that we will drag "from" and "to". By examining the source code, we can see that we want to drag is called, "draggable" and the one we want to make the drop at is called "droppable". We'll use these IDs (not NAMES this time) in the code below to create drag-able and drop-able objects.

```
#---------------------------
# startof: drag and drop

# Locate page elements
elementDraggable = driver.find_element(By.ID, "draggable")
elementDroppable = driver.find_element(By.ID, "droppable")

libBot.writeLog(logFile, "Starting drag and drop")
actions = ActionChains(driver)
libBot.randomWait(logFile, 2, 3)

libBot.writeLog(logFile, "Drag draggable into droppable")
actions.drag_and_drop(elementDraggable, elementDroppable).perform()

libBot.randomWait(logFile, 2, 3)
```

Script 8.3, Performing the first "drag-and-drop"

The next step is to instantiate the ActionChains object. Once we have that, placing the draggable object into the droppable object is done with a single command, executed by a `perform()` method.

A (smooth) drag and drop

The only problem with the approach above is that the draggable box instantaneously transports to it's destination with no time interval in between. This might be efficacious, but it does not follow our rule that bots should look people. And regardless how fast your mouse hand is, no one can do an instantaneous drag-and-drop. It's not humanly possible.

The way we implement a more human-looking "smooth drag-and-drop" is by employing the ActionChains method that allows us to move a web object (objectively, we're moving the mouse) with an offset. If you put that offset in a loop you can obtain a smooth(ish) move from one location to another, as depicted in the code segment below.

```
#--------------------------
# startof: "smooth" drag and drop

# Locate page elements
elementDraggable = driver.find_element(By.ID, "draggable")
elementDroppable = driver.find_element(By.ID, "droppable")
libBot.writeLog(logFile, "Starting drag and drop")
actions = ActionChains(driver)
libBot.randomWait(logFile, 2, 3)

libBot.writeLog(logFile, "(Smoothly) drag draggable into droppable")
for x in range(3, 30):
        xPos = x*(0.40)
        yPos = x*(0.20)
        libBot.writeLog(logFile, "xPos:" + str(xPos) + ", yPos:" + str(yPos) )
        actions.move_to_element(elementDraggable).click_and_hold().move_by_offset(xPos,
yPos).release().perform()

libBot.randomWait(logFile, 2, 3)

libBot.writeLog(logFile, "Return to the main frame and scroll to the bottom.")
driver.switch_to.default_content()
```

Script 8.4 Implementing a "smooth drag-and-drop"

While this approach is smoother, it's not perfect. But it's an improvement over instantaneously transporting objects around the web page. I'd recommend something like Script 8.3, but with randomness in the positioning loop.

Controlling a JQuery slider

You'll notice some similarity between controlling the slider with the drag-and-drop examples. For example, the find_element method to locate the web object, and ActionChains is used to manipulate it.

```
#----------------------------
# startof: slider
libBot.writeLog(logFile, "Start slider")

# Locate the slider element
slider = driver.find_element(By.ID, 'slider')

# Use ActionChains to move the slider
actions = ActionChains(driver)
libBot.writeLog(logFile, "move slider")

libBot.writeLog(logFile, "offset: 126")

actions.move_to_element(slider).click_and_hold().move_by_offset(126, 0).release().perform()
libBot.randomWait(logFile, 2, 3)
```

Script 8.5, Moving slider controls

And like the example that came immediately before this example, moving a slider also requires that we use the offset to move the slider a required distance, as shown above.

ActionChains commonalities

By now, parts of ActionChains should start to look predictable, if not familiar. The things that characterize ActionChains, up to this point, include:

1. Identifying the involved web elements (with find_element),

2. Creating an ActionChains object (from the driver),

3. Creating a chain of actions that can include, various mouse function, and

4. Using the perform() method to execute the chain of actions.

Controlling a JQuery date picker

The code that is used to control the JQuery date picker is included here because—not only does it show how to control a data picker, but because it demonstrates the fact that complicated custom controls often have simple overrides. In this case, we can completely avoid the act of selecting the year, month and day on a calendar and simple write the value we want into a text box, as shown in the script segment below.

```
#---------------------------
# startof: date picker
libBot.randomWait(logFile, 8, 9)
libBot.writeLog(logFile, "Start date picker")
driver.find_element(By.ID, "datepicker").click()
libBot.randomWait(logFile, 2, 3)
driver.find_element(By.ID, "datepicker").send_keys("07/04/2023")
libBot.randomWait(logFile, 2, 3)
```

Script 8.6, Controlling a JQuery data picker

Since a human user of the date picker has the same option of hand-entering the date, this shouldn't be looked at as something that might bring attention to our bot.

There was a time when I always used the Selenium IDE to figure out how to control custom controls like the ones shown in this project. This is, in fact, the only use for the IDE that I was able to justify. Once I understood how ActionChains worked, however, I never used the Selenium IDE again. The reality is that none of this is that hard to learn, and it's liberating to free oneself of tools one doesn't need.

Script: actionChains.py

```
########################################################################
scriptName = "actionChains" + ".py"
# My (personal) path for this file
#--------------------------

# # # # # # # # # # # # # #
# Configuration
import   sys
import   os
import   time

from     datetime import   datetime
from     random   import   randint

import   selenium
from     selenium.webdriver.common.by                        import By

from     selenium.webdriver.common.keys                    import Keys
from     selenium.webdriver.common.action_chains    import ActionChains

# # # # # # # # # # # # # #
# Record the start time
start_time = time.time()
timeStart = datetime.today().strftime('%Y%m%d_%H%M%S')

# # # # # # # # # # # # # #
# Establish paths and import libraries
#
sys.path.insert(0, "../../libs")          # Import local libraries
from libPaths              import logFile
from libPaths              import pathChromeDriver

import libBot              # Useful bot functions

import libParse            # Parse functions

from libParse              import BEFORE
from libParse              import AFTER

import libSelenium         # Selenium (chromedriver) specific functions


# # # # # # # # # # # # # #
# Manage Logs
try:
        os.system("del *.log")
except:
        libBot.writeLog(logFile, "There were no log files to remove.")

print("\n")
libBot.writeLog(logFile, "###########################################")
```

100

```
libBot.writeLog(logFile, "# " + scriptName)
libBot.writeLog(logFile, "##########################################")
libBot.writeLog(logFile, "Log file: " + logFile)

# Load Selenium (get driver) and resize/reposition the browser window
driver = libSelenium.loadWebdriver(logFile, pathChromeDriver)
libSelenium.setWindowSize(logFile, driver, x=800, y=300)
libSelenium.setWindowPosition(logFile, driver, x=10, y=10)

########################################################################
########################################################################
## Start: PAYLOAD (This is where the work is performed.)
##
try:
        driver.get("http://mepso.com/publishing/selenium_python/examples/customControls/")
        driver.set_window_size(900, 875)
        time.sleep(2)

        #---------------------------
        # startof: drag and drop

        # Locate page elements
        elementDraggable = driver.find_element(By.ID, "draggable")
        elementDroppable = driver.find_element(By.ID, "droppable")

        libBot.writeLog(logFile, "Starting drag and drop")
        actions = ActionChains(driver)
        libBot.randomWait(logFile, 2, 3)

        libBot.writeLog(logFile, "Drag draggable into droppable")
        actions.drag_and_drop(elementDraggable, elementDroppable).perform()

        libBot.randomWait(logFile, 2, 3)

        #---------------------------
        # start of: "smooth" drag and drop

        # Switch to frame
        driver.switch_to.default_content()
        libBot.randomWait(logFile, 2, 3)
        driver.switch_to.frame('exampleFrame')

        # Locate page elements
        elementDraggable = driver.find_element(By.ID, "draggable")
        elementDroppable = driver.find_element(By.ID, "droppable")

        libBot.writeLog(logFile, "Starting drag and drop")
        actions = ActionChains(driver)
        libBot.randomWait(logFile, 2, 3)

        libBot.writeLog(logFile, "(Smoothly) drag draggable into droppable")
        for x in range(3, 30):
                xPos = x*(0.40)
```

```python
                yPos = x*(0.20)
                libBot.writeLog(logFile, "xPos:" + str(xPos) + ", yPos:" + str(yPos) )

        actions.move_to_element(elementDraggable).click_and_hold().move_by_offset(xPos,
yPos).release().perform()

        libBot.randomWait(logFile, 2, 3)

        libBot.writeLog(logFile, "Return to the main frame and scroll to the bottom.")
        driver.switch_to.default_content()

        #---------------------------
        # start of: slider
        libBot.writeLog(logFile, "Start slider")

        # Locate the slider element
        slider = driver.find_element(By.ID, 'slider')

        # Use ActionChains to move the slider
        actions = ActionChains(driver)
        libBot.writeLog(logFile, "move slider")

        libBot.writeLog(logFile, "offset: 126")
        actions.move_to_element(slider).click_and_hold().move_by_offset(126,
0).release().perform()
        libBot.randomWait(logFile, 2, 3)

        #---------------------------
        # start of: date picker
        libBot.randomWait(logFile, 8, 9)
        libBot.writeLog(logFile, "Start date picker")
        driver.find_element(By.ID, "datepicker").click()
        libBot.randomWait(logFile, 2, 3)
        driver.find_element(By.ID, "datepicker").send_keys("07/04/2023")
        libBot.randomWait(logFile, 7, 8)
        libBot.writeLog(logFile, "Calendar complete")

except:
        libBot.closeBot(logFile, driver, "Unable to open website")

libBot.randomWait(logFile, 7, 9)


# ENDOF Payload
########################################################################
########################################################################

# # # # # # # # # # # # # #
# Close gracefully
libBot.closeBot(logFile, driver, "Exiting normally: "+scriptName)
########################################################################
```

## CHAPTER 9

PROJ 06: PARSING AND AGGREGATION

If you write bots for any length of time, you'll probably be asked to develop bots that collect data from multiple—but different, sources and in multiple formats. The trick is to collect the data, find commonalities, and store the data from each independent source into one common format file that consolidates the data from all sources.

This example bot describes three separate ways to parse disparate data from multiple sources and to format the collected data into a common format for transmission to another service for processing.

The CSV file, created by this bot, is uploaded later in a process described in Chapter 22, *"Big Data is a Big Headache"*.

This project also involves a good deal of parsing. Please note that the parsing theory discussed here is really only intended to get you started on this particular project. There is much more parsing theory in Chapter 18, *"Parsing text and the semantic web"*.

Watch the associated video on YouTube

 The video for this project, especially the code walk-through is a real supplement to the book. I think this is because it's easier to consume a code walk-through as a video than a text. And this code review is fairly lengthly.

Figure 9.1, Chapter video

Big chucks or little chunks?

We obviously collect data with the purpose of using it somewhere. It could be anywhere, but it's most likely not where it was collected. The assumption is that it will need to be written to a remote database. So we need to ask ourselves, "What is the best way to move data collected by bots?" Should we move it as it's collected (with many server connections) or wait until the data collection for that task was completed and upload all the data with with one big server connection?

In one case, about ten years ago, I was collecting a lot of individual records from a website. At the time, I decided to upload every record as they became available, in contrast to collecting data and storing in a larger collection for later uploading. My logic was that fresh data was better than old data, so I intended to get the data to the server as quickly as possible. In that application, I used over fifty bots to gather data from around ten sources. These bots ran every minute and would upload around fifty records per cycle. For those of you, who are doing that math in your head, that's fifty bots each uploading fifty records every minute, or 2500 connections a minute. This was complicated by the fact that these connections came from a limited number of IP addresses

This approach, of uploading data as soon as it was available, was working great. My main concern was that the central server—that was accepting all these connections and writing data to a database, was not going to be able to keep up with all that activity. But it was purring along fine without consuming too many resources.

It wasn't long, however, before I got a message from the web host saying that my website was under attack and they blocked the IP addresses of my bots to protect *their* network. They (a web host I still value and will not mention) thought they were protecting me from a *DDOS*, or a Distributed Denial of Service Attack. It's hard to get upset with people that are trying to protect you. So there was no reason to try to justify what I was doing to them. It was easier to reevaluate my approach.

It was here that I started to favor collecting data into a larger CSV file, and uploading a collection of data at once. How long you wait to upload the CSV file is determined by how important it is to have fresh data. In most cases, compromises are unnoticed, and I found that bots put much less stress on the system by uploading compiled data instead of individual records.

Standardized data communications

The other magical thing about formatted CSV files is that they make it much easier to upload data. This is because you can write a universal API that can accept any collection of data into a database, as long as the column headers of an uploaded CSV file matched the column names of a database. The alternative, is to document, develop, debug, and deploy a new API every time you want to transfer some data. I don't know about you, but I have better things to do with my time.

For example, the following CSV file has a header that directly matches the table it is written to on a remote server.

```
NAME_FIRST, NAME_LAST, ADDRESS, CITY, STATE, ZIP
JILL, MONROE, 3423 Lilac Drive, Golden Valley, MN, 55423
SABRINA, DUNCAN, 1932 Clarendon Avenue, Los Angeles, CA 98434
KELLY, GARRETT, One Main Street, Tonapah, NV, 89117
```

Script 9.1, A file formatted to match the database schema

When a data file has the same format as the database table it intends to write to, a universal API can be written that essentially just needs to write (or update) data to the fields described in the file header.

```
NAME_FIRST      VARCHAR(50)
NAME_LAST       VARCHAR(50)
ADDRESS         VARCHAR(250)
CITY            VARCHAR(150)
STATE           CHAR(2)
ZIP             CHAR(10)
```

Script 9.2, The corresponding database table

This technique has saved me countless hours, and makes transferring data much easier. Now I only have to write one API, secure it, and reuse it over and over. There is much more to say about how I use CSV files in *Chapter 22, "Big data, big headache"*.

The targets

This example gets data from three data sources. Each source has similar data, but in different formats. And each will have to be parsed differently depending on their format.

Each of the targets uses data that is both randomized in content and in quantity. So, no source will have the same data twice.

The first data set is a straight forward set of tabulated data. This will be very easy to parse into a formatted file.

#	First Name	Last Name	Street 1	Street 2	City	State	Postal Code
1.	Amber	Bertrand	8504 George Freeway		Northampton	DE	19701
2.	Brianna	Lamontagne	6147 Woodland Freeway	Unit 16	Stirling	LA	70001
3.	Evelyn	Charron	4580 The Crescent Street	No. 8	Edinburgh	CA	90001
4.	Poppy	Caron	6751 Elm Street		Swansea	HI	96701
5.	Annabelle	Allen	6876 88th Avenue	No. 6	Middlesbrough	TX	73301
6.	Catriona	Hébert	4439 The Close Street	Apartment 8		DE	19701
7.	Carys	Dupont	5817 Market Way		Salford	TN	37010
8.	Jake	Franklin	7214 10th Street	Apartment 12	Perth	AR	71601
9.	Thomas	Gray	983 Bridge Way	No. 10	Guildford	OK	73001
10.	Riley	Henry	2899 Manor Highway		Nottingham	NY	0501
11.	Jake	Ward	61 68th Street	Unit 18	Luton	NH	03031
12.	Henry	Caron	9908 Park Interchange	Unit 11	Swindon	ND	58001
13.	Amelia	Desrochers	4599 94th Street		Derby	NY	0501
14.	Toby	James	15 The Drive Plaza	No. 3	Wigan	WY	82001
15.	Alexander	Smith	1035 24th Street	Apt 15	Plymouth	TX	73301
16.	Alastair	Guilbault	9529 North Interchange		Stockport	NE	68001
17.	Caroline	Davis	6604 Sycamore Highway	Unit 2	Stoke	TX	73301
18.	Alice	Ford	2700 29th Street	No. 3	Kingston upon Hull	IN	46001
19.	Alexandra	Boucher	109 77th Street		Ipswich	TX	73301
20.	Carmen	Parker	9938 Ashton Avenue	Apt 22	Northampton	WV	24701
21.	Cameron	Garza	4522 28th Street	Apt 1	Leicester	OR	97001
22.	Jacob	Harper	3642 The Drive Boulevard		Cheltenham	CO	80001
23.	Amelia	Fuller	3659 North Place	Apartment 7	Wolverhampton	MO	63005
24.	Noah	Couture	1214 Hillside Avenue	Unit 2	Inverness	UT	84001
25.	Carla	Brault	8885 Woodland Boulevard		Manchester	MN	55001

SALES GROUP A: FINAL ON WEEK OF 2023-06-20

Figure 9.2, The first dataset

With this source, we will treat the data like the table data it is. In other words, we will first parse the table rows, and then parse the table cells within those table rows.

The second data set is fairly similar to the first, but the First and Last Names are truncated to their initial, either for privacy or space reasons. Notice, however, that the full first and last names are available when the mouse hovers over the initials, as shown in Figure 9.3. This will be a little harder to parse than the first dataset.

Sales on Jun, 27, 2023

Member	Street 1	City	State	Postal Code
C. B	8888 Market Way	Halifax	CO	80001
A. S	7150 South Plaza, No. 12	Gloucester	AL	35004
A. L	5652 Mill Freeway, Apt 8	Perth	KY	40003
P. C	4076 Baker Boulevard	Winchester	LA	70001
S. B	6152 Elm Boulevard, Apt 20	Oldham	IN	46001
C. E	1909 Market Street, No. 8	Milton Keynes	MD	20601
E. M	8782 The Close Place	Luton	UT	84001
A. B	7686 58th Avenue, Apt 22	Carlisle	ID	83201
R. H	2540 10th Street, Unit 13	Ipswich	TN	37010
E. D	1278 37th Street	Bath	ME	03901
I. H	3040 The Crescent Street, No. 10	Coventry	KY	40003
A. B	8707 Orchard Freeway, Apartment 16	Brighton	NE	68001

(Cassandra Bouchard — tooltip over A. S / A. L rows)

Figure 9.3, The second dataset

We'll parse this data differently than the last example, with a technique that has become one of my favorite ways to parse tablature data.

And finally we have the third dataset, which is completely unformatted and looks like it was developed in the age of the fax machine.

```
SALES GROUP A: FINAL ON WEEK OF 2023-06-21
1      Name:Joshua Taylor      Street: 7877 The Drive Avenue
          City/State: Swansea, OK 73001
2      Name:Bruce Hicks        Street: 4453 King Boulevard
       Address:    Apartment 16    City/State: Inverness, ND 58001
3      Name:Ruby King        Street: 4452 Oak Interchange
       Address:    No. 2    City/State: Harrogate, CA 90001
4      Name:Elijah Ellis       Street: 1878 Springfield Plaza
          City/State: Southampton, CA 90001
5      Name:Edward Fowler      Street: 2566 East Interchange
       Address:    Apartment 19    City/State: Carlisle, NC 27006
6      Name:Austin Edwards      Street: 3525 North Boulevard
       Address:    Apartment 20    City/State: Swansea, LA 70001
7      Name:Alexandra Collins      Street: 4005 74th Street
          City/State: Grimsby, MS 38601
8      Name:Bruce Bourgeois      Street: 7443 East Avenue
       Address:    Unit 17    City/State: Newcastle upon Tyne, TN 37010
9      Name:Catherine Simpson      Street: 1805 George Way
       Address:    Unit 19    City/State: Milton Keynes, WI 53001
10     Name:Thomas Brisson      Street: 4040 60th Street
          City/State: Blackburn, RI 02801
11     Name:Matthew Lafontaine      Street: 3124 Elm Avenue
       Address:    Apartment 21    City/State: Cheltenham, WI 53001
12     Name:Bruce Dunn      Street: 9066 Main Boulevard
       Address:    Apt 17    City/State: Armagh, IL 60001
13     Name:Lucy Chapman      Street: 4217 36th Avenue
          City/State: Poole, MT 59001
14     Name:Clara Fuller      Street: 3824 19th Avenue
       Address:    Apartment 12    City/State: Preston, NJ 07001
15     Name:Celeste Edwards      Street: 1152 80th Street
       Address:    Apartment 16    City/State: Belfast, NY 0501
16     Name:Nina Lewis      Street: 814 Market Interchange
          City/State: Kingston upon Hull, MI 48001
17     Name:Beatrice Walker      Street: 360 Cedar Place
       Address:    Apt 3    City/State: Southport, CA 90001
18     Name:Bruce Griffiths      Street: 8813 Willow Boulevard
       Address:    No. 14    City/State: Stockport, VA 20101
19     Name:Bryony Hall      Street: 3057 66th Street
          City/State: Bradford, MO 63005
20     Name:Lucas Gomez      Street: 5786 South Highway
       Address:    Apt 8    City/State: Swansea, VA 20101
21     Name:Oliver Burton      Street: 1258 31th Avenue
       Address:    Apartment 14    City/State: Oxford, ND 58001
22     Name:Aimee Beauchamp      Street: 7638 Green Way
          City/State: Gloucester, AK 99501
23     Name:Cassandra Brault      Street: 7742 68th Street
       Address:    Apartment 7    City/State: Wolverhampton, FL 32003
```

Figure 9.4, The third collection with an unformatted, dataset.

Planning a parsing approach

The first two datasets will be easily parsed because of their grid nature. In the case of tables, each row represents one complete data record and the cells within those rows determine the parameters that correspond to the values in the cells. So for these examples, the parsers will attempt to build arrays from the table tows, and then define indexes to reference the cells within those rows.

The second dataset will need to parse the associated first and last names in each data record. And while this adds an extra step, it is not a difficult thing to do.

The third dataset sill be more difficult to parse because if has no real format. In those cases, it is often useful to instill our own format to more easily parse the content.

Selecting a format

While this book makes extensive use of CSV files, you shouldn't see that as any limitation to what you do. You could use other standardized formats like, JSON or XML if you like—or come up with a proprietary one of your own. As long as you're consistent, and the data fields match those of your database table, you'll be fine. The reason CSV files were chosen for this book is due to their simplicity and universal use. Additionally, there are tools (Excel, LibreOffice, Google Docs, etc.) available to easily validate that the data and format of the file are correct.

It is very common to find extended character sets on websites. If you're storing web data to a database, you may want to convert all data to UTF-8, or the character format that your database uses. Otherwise, you may experience data loss.

The aggregation plan

The assumption is that the bot will upload the data to a centralized server. to do that, data from all three parses will be aggregated in a common, formatted file. This file could be in any format, as long as the accompanying API on the server can accommodate it. And while this file could be in any format, including XML, or JSON, I choose CSV because it most closely resembles a database table. And I find that visual reference both assuring and familiar.

Code Walk-through

Like the others, this project uses the framework developed in Project 2. As such, we will again only focus on the payload of the framework.

The first steep is to download the web page where the first dateset is. Please keep in mind that we're taking an extremely streamlined approach for the sake of clarity. In real life, you may have to navigate through a series of pages, complete authentication or solve a CAPTCHA.

```
###########################################################################
# Get first source

# Download the page
libBot.writeLog(logFile, "Getting the first source.")
domain = "https://mepso.com/"
path = "publishing/selenium_python/examples/parseAggregation/group1.php"
libBot.writeLog(logFile, "Getting: " + domain+path)
driver.get(domain+path)
libBot.randomWait(logFile, 2, 3)
```

Script 9.3 Downloading the first dataset

The script, as shown above, downloads the first dataset. Once the page is displayed in the browser we can begin parsing it.

In the script below, you can see that a table identified as "orders" is the subject of a JavaScript routine that obtains the contents of the data. This data is stored in the variable `tableHTML`. This isn't the first time we've used Selenium to execute arbitrary code on the target website. But it's worth reminding ourselves of the power of Selenium, and that this is even feasible.

```
# Separate the text to parse from everything else
tableHTML = driver.execute_script("return document.getElementById('orders').innerHTML;")
```
Script 9.4 Putting the table contents into a variable

Now that the table data is in a single variable, it's a good time to do any processing that will affect all the data. In this case, it was decided that all " " should be removed, as shown below.

```
tableHTML = libParse.strReplace(" ", "", tableHTML)
```
Script 9.5, Removing all non-breaking spaces

110

The next step is to build an array where each array element holds one complete data record. We do this by using the `parseArray()` function in libParse, as shown below.

```
ArrRows = libParse.parseArray(tableHTML, "<tr", "</tr>", EXCL)
```

Script 9.6, Converting table rows into an array

Once the complete dataset is contained in an array, where each row in the array represents each row in the table, it's a simple matter of looping through the array. At each loop iteration:

- A variable `thisRow` is assigned the current table row,

- Some housekeeping is done. In this case, any line feeds within the row are removed.

- The table row's data cells are parsed into an array, `ArrCells`, of table cells, as shown in the following script segment.

```
for row in range(1, len(ArrRows)):
        thisRow = ArrRows[row]
        thisRow = libParse.strReplace("\n", "", thisRow)
        ArrCells = libParse.parseArray(thisRow, "<td ", "</td>", INCL)
```

Script 9.7, parsing the rows in the first dataset

The final step in parsing the first dataset is to move the values into the CSV file. But before that is done, the CSV array is initiated to null values with the desired index. Transferring data from one array is an easy thing to do as the data now exists in array elements. Array element 0 is assigned to the current time. The others are stripped of any residual HTML characters. The address cell (cell 3) goes through a manipulation that removes all redundant spaces.

An eighth element is added to show which data group this data belongs to, and the data is written to the CSV file with the write CSV function.

```
        csv = ["", "", "", "", "", "", "", "", ""]
        csv[0]   = timeStart

        for cell in range(1, 8):
```

```
                csv[cell] = libParse.stripTags(ArrCells[cell]).strip()

        # Go back and clean-up the address cell
        csv[3] = libParse.stripTags(ArrCells[3])
        csv[3] = libParse.strReplace("  ", "~", csv[3])
        csv[3] = libParse.strReplace("~", "", csv[3])

        # Add group
        csv[8]   = "Group 1"

        libBot.writeLog(logFile, "Writing line to CSV file")
        writeCSV(logFile, "test.csv", csv)

libBot.randomWait(logFile, 2, 3)

# endOf Get first source
#--------------------------------
```
Script 9.8, Transferring the first dataset to the CSV file

Parsing the second dataset

The second data set is very much like the first; the only difference being that the name was somewhat protected by only showing the first and second initial. This means that the full first and last name will have to be parsed from the title attribute of the link that's present. The page is downloaded with the code in Script 9.9.

```
#######################################################################
# Get second source

# Download the page
libBot.writeLog(logFile, "Getting the second source.")
domain = "http://mepso.com/"
path = "publishing/selenium_python/examples/parseAggregation/group2.php"
libBot.writeLog(logFile, "Getting: " + domain+path)
driver.get(domain+path)
libBot.randomWait(logFile, 2, 3)
```
Script 9.9, downloading the second source

 Like the first data set, this data is in table form. But, we're going to us a much more Selenium-esque technique for extracting table data. This is actually my favorite approach for extracting data of this type. This parse also works well in areas with you have data of unknown length, like this example.

112

The key difference between parsing this dataset and the one that came prior is that this one is parsed with `find_element(By.XPATH).`

This might be a good time to skip ahead and visit *Chapter 16, Locators*, for a look at how XPATH works as a locator. We stumbled into XPATH in Project 4, where it was used to identify options in a select list.

Here, we use XPATH is an identifier just like ID and NAME. Again, it might be worth while to skip ahead to Chapters 15 and 16 for more information on the Document Object Model and Selenium Locators.

This parse works like this. Since XPATH is essentially an array that describe a webpage, XPATH will have array elements that represent table rows and columns. So, by looping through the rows and columns—as represented by XPATH, we should be able to capture all the data in the table.

The code in Script 9.10, we create a loop that is longer than the number of rows we anticipate to be in the table. There is no reason not to use a number larger than the one I chose (40).

```
maxRows = 40
for row in range(2, maxRows):
        '''
        STARTof: Table XPATH
        # First line in table
        /html/body/table/tbody/tr[2]/td[1]
        /html/body/table/tbody/tr[2]/td[2]
        /html/body/table/tbody/tr[2]/td[3]
        /html/body/table/tbody/tr[2]/td[3]
        /html/body/table/tbody/tr[2]/td[5]
        # Second line in table
        /html/body/table/tbody/tr[3]/td[1]
        /html/body/table/tbody/tr[3]/td[3]
        /html/body/table/tbody/tr[3]/td[2]...
        ENDof: Table XPATH
        '''
```

Script 9.10, Loop initiation

The commented code above, in Script 9.10, also shows what the XPATH for part of the table looks like. This might not make total sense to you, but recognize for now that

XPATH is an array. And that the XPATH above defines the first full data row (row 2) and that the table cells iterate from 1 to 5. (XPATH arrays start at element 1, not 0.) The second line of XPATH definitions for the next row is identical to the earlier one, except that the row is incremented (to 3).

I used Chrome Inspect *(Chapter 23)* to determine what the XPATH values. Chapter 23 is devoted to Chrome Inspect, so plan on getting the details there.

Earlier, you read that we are creating a loop that is larger than the number of records we anticipate to find in Source Two. We do this, obviously, not to miss any of the data, and to be prepared for more data that we expect. We know when we're done because python will raise an exception when we reference data that doesn't exist.

In Script 9.11, we can see that our attempts to read the table are subject to some Python exception handling. If we fail to find any of the web elements (table cells) we're looking for, we fall through to the except handler that basically says we're done parsing the table.

```
try:
        # parse name from initials
        xpathTxt =  "/html/body/table/tbody/tr["+str(row)+"]/td[1]"
        temp = driver.find_element(By.XPATH, xpathTxt)
        nameHTML = temp.get_attribute("innerHTML")

        nameFirst = libParse.returnBetween(nameHTML, 'title="', '&', EXCL)
        nameLast = libParse.returnBetween(nameHTML, ' ', '"', EXCL)
```

Script 9.11, Initiating the exception handling and getting the first table cell

Again, there's more JavaScript looking stuff here. Once we use Selenium to locate the table cell of interest (the one with the initials), we gather the `innerHTML` attribute to get the contents of the cell. Notice that this is different than how we extract the data for the other cells. In this cell, we need the actual HTML because we have to parse the first and last names from the title attribute in a link. For the other table cells, we don't need or want HTML so we ask for the `text` instead of `innerHTML` attribute.

```
        # Street (1 and 2)
        xpathTxt =  "/html/body/table/tbody/tr["+str(row)+"]/td[2]"
        street = driver.find_element(By.XPATH, xpathTxt).text
        if libParse.stristr(street, ","):
                street1 = libParse.splitString(street, ",", BEFORE, EXCL)
```

114

```
                         street2 = libParse.splitString(street, ",", AFTER, EXCL)
              else:
                         street1 = libParse.stripTags(street).strip()
                         street2 = ""

              # city
              xpathTxt =   "/html/body/table/tbody/tr["+str(row)+"]/td[3]"
              city = driver.find_element(By.XPATH, xpathTxt).text

              # state
              xpathTxt =   "/html/body/table/tbody/tr["+str(row)+"]/td[4]"
              state = driver.find_element(By.XPATH, xpathTxt).text

              # postalCode
              xpathTxt =   "/html/body/table/tbody/tr["+str(row)+"]/td[5]"
              postalCode = driver.find_element(By.XPATH, xpathTxt).text
```

Script 9.12, Parsing the data cells

Once the data for a full row is collected, that data is loaded into an array, called CSV, where the elements are arranged as shown in Script 9.13.

```
              # write to CSV file
              csv = initCSV()
              csv[0]   = timeStart
              csv[1]   = nameFirst
              csv[2]   = nameLast
              csv[3]   = street1
              csv[4]   = street2
              csv[5]   = city
              csv[6]   = state
              csv[7]   = postalCode.strip()
              csv[8]   = "Group 2"
              libBot.writeLog(logFile, "Writing line to CSV file")
              writeCSV(logFile, "test.csv", csv)
      except:
              print("We found the last row")
              break

# endOf Get second source
```

Script 9.13 Loading the data into the CSV file.

As before, the function `writeCSV()`[5] will check to see if the csv file exists. If it does, it will append this data to the end of the CSV file. Otherwise, it will write the header row first.

Parsing the third dataset

The third dataset starts like the other two, by downloading the associated web page, as shown below. And like the other two, the URL you're using is later redirected to the actual location.

```
###################################################################
# Get third source

# Download the page
libBot.writeLog(logFile, "Getting the second source.")
url= "http://mepso.com/exp/SP2_6c.php"
libBot.writeLog(logFile, "Getting: " + url)
driver.get(irl)
libBot.randomWait(logFile, 2, 3)
```

Script 9.10, Downloading the third source

And that's where comparisons to the other two sources ends. This source lacks the structure that the other two inherited from being in tables. So, this parse will be more complex. But regardless of the complexity, the idea of creating an array that holds the data records is still valid. But we will have to create the structure though something I call the insertion parse[6].

The insertion parse makes parsing easier by inserting tags into the text, at places were you want to differentiate one record from another. For example, I know I want a terminal tag at the end of the data, so I insert a "`</tag>`" tag at the end of the data, as shown below.

```
# Separate the text to parse from everything else
html = libBot.getWebpageContents(logFile, driver) + "</tag>"
html = libParse.strReplace("Name:", "</tag><tag>", html)
ArrOrders = libParse.parseArray(html, "<tag>", "</tag>", EXCL)
```

---

5 There is more information on writeCSV() near the end of this chapter.

6 The "insertion parse" was introduced in my first book, "Webbots, Spiders, and Screen Scrapers", No Starch Press 2007.

Once that terminal tag is in place, I identified a constant place that separates one record from the next. In this case, the text, `Name:` serves that purpose. Replacing that text with a pair of tags, "`</tag><tag>`", ensures that each data record is prefixed by "`<tag>`", and closed with a "`</tag>`". Once the records have the appropriate bookends, they are easily parsed into arrays, much like the prior datasets and processed in a loop, as on the next page.

```
for row in range(0, len(ArrOrders)):

    name = libParse.splitString(ArrOrders[row], "Street:", BEFORE, EXCL)
    street = libParse.returnBetween(ArrOrders[row], "Street:", "\n", EXCL)

    if libParse.stristr(ArrOrders[row], "Address:"):
        street2 = libParse.returnBetween(ArrOrders[row], "Address:", "City/State:", EXCL)
    else:
        street2 = ""

    cityStateZip = libParse.splitString(ArrOrders[row], "State:", AFTER, EXCL)
    stateZip = libParse.returnBetween(cityStateZip, ",", "\n", EXCL).strip()
    city = libParse.splitString(cityStateZip, ",", BEFORE, EXCL)
    state = libParse.splitString(stateZip, " ", BEFORE, EXCL)
    zipCode = libParse.splitString(stateZip, " ", AFTER, EXCL)
```

Script 9.12, Parsing unformatted data.

Unlike the other two datasets, here we cannot produce an indexed array of the record. So the individual data values must be individually parsed. Most of these parses are performed with libParse's `returnBetween()`, or other similar parse function.

Once the data is defined, it is placed into the csv array with the data order the same as it was for the previous two datasets, as shown below.

```
csv = initCSV()
csv[0] = timeStart
csv[1] = libParse.splitString(name, " ", BEFORE, EXCL).strip()
csv[2] = libParse.splitString(name, " ", AFTER, EXCL).strip()
csv[3] = street.strip()
csv[4] = street2.strip()

csv[5] = city
csv[6] = state
csv[7] = zipCode
csv[8] = "Group 3"
```

117

```
        libBot.writeLog(logFile, "Writing line to CSV file")
        writeCSV(logFile, "test.csv", csv)

# endOf Get third source
#--------------------------------
```

Script 9.13, Moving the third dataset into the CSV file.

At this point, all three datasets have been parsed and placed into a single CSV file.

	A	B	C	D	E	F	G	H	I
1	DATE	NAME_FIRST	NAME_LAST	STREET_1	STREET_2	CITY	STATE	POSTAL_CODE	GROUP
2	20230524_193653	Jacob	Clark	156 Chestnut Interchange		Plymouth	OK	73001	Group 1
3	20230524_193653	Carmen	James	4083 Victoria Highway	Apartment 2	Bolton	NM	87001	Group 1
4	20230524_193653	Jasmine	Wilson	8844 Baker Boulevard	Apt 1	Coventry	TN	37010	Group 1
5	20230524_193653	Archie	Franklin	732 96th Avenue		Cheltenham	NH	3031	Group 1
6	20230524_193653	Ruby	Curry	4990 85th Avenue	Apt 12	Stockport	KS	66002	Group 1
7	20230524_193653	Carl	Freeman	7052 34th Street		Salford	NE	68001	Group 2
8	20230524_193653	Amelie	Desrochers	2467 North Place	Apartment 3	Dundee	MS	38601	Group 2
9	20230524_193653	Ruby	Ferguson	7454 Manor Avenue	No. 14	Salford	AK	99501	Group 2
10	20230524_193653	Harriet	Gutierrez	6741 Cedar Avenue		Liverpool	OH	43001	Group 2
11	20230524_193653	Caitlin	Edwards	1834 Queen Highway	No. 1	Milton Keynes	KS	66002	Group 2
12	20230524_193653	Eva	Taylor	9956 50th Street	No. 1	Bolton	MT	59001	Group 2
13	20230524_193653	Henry	Gaudreau	4738 Springfield Way	Apt 1	Swansea	PA	15001	Group 3
14	20230524_193653	Brendan	Ford	1298 Baker Freeway	No. 3	Lancaster	ND	58001	Group 3
15	20230524_193653	Aimee	Leduc	1857 Hillside Freeway		Bolton	HI	96701	Group 3
16	20230524_193653	Daniel	Gauthier	935 Station Avenue	Apartment 4	Lancaster	WA	98001	Group 3
17	20230524_193653	Charlotte	Legault	4937 The Avenue Plaza	No. 11	Bangor	CO	80001	Group 3

Figure 9.14 The resulting CSV file (truncated)

A truncated version of the CSV file is shown above for reference.

The writeCSV() function

What hasn't been mentioned is how the CSV file is actually created. Each of the datasets relied on the writeCSV() function, which is shown below.

```
#--------------------------------
def writeCSV(logFile, fileName, array):
        header = ''
        header =  header + '"DATE", "NAME_FIRST", "NAME_LAST", "STREET_1", '
        header =  header + '"STREET_2", "CITY", "STATE", "POSTAL_CODE", "GROUP"\n'

        # if file doesn't exist, write the header
        if not os.path.isfile(fileName):
                libBot.writeLog(logFile, "Creating new CSV file")
                libBot.writeFile(logFile, fileName, header)

        # write the array into the csv file
        csv = ""
        for data in array:
                csv = csv + '"'+data.strip()+'", '
```

118

```
        libBot.appendFile(logFile, fileName, csv+"\n")

#------------------------------------
```

Script 9.14, The writeCSV() function.

The `writeCSV()` function does the following:

1. Defines the header, where the header labels are identical to the column names in a corresponding database table,

2. If the CSV file doesn't exist, it will create it.

3. The data is written and encased in quotes.

4. Each line is terminated with a linefeed (`"\n"`).

As mentioend earlier, this type of project is task you will do repeatedly if you develop bots for datacollection. So, it's a good idea to get into good habits and pick a dataformat and stick with it. You'll have much mor time for creative work if you can standardize the routine stuff.

Script: parseAggregate.py

```
######################################################################
scriptName = "parseAggregate" + ".py"
#--------------------------

# # # # # # # # # # # # # #
# Configuration
import  sys
import  os
import  time

from    datetime        import datetime
from    random          import  randint

import  selenium
from     selenium.webdriver.common.by import By
from     selenium.webdriver.common.keys import Keys

# # # # # # # # # # # # # #
# Record the start time
start_time = time.time()
timeStart = datetime.today().strftime('%Y%m%d_%H%M%S')

# # # # # # # # # # # # # #
# Establish paths and import libraries
#
sys.path.insert(0, "../../libs")          # Import local libraries
from     libPaths        import logFile
from     libPaths        import pathChromeDriver
from     libPaths        import pathRoot

import   libBot          # Useful bot functions

import   libParse # Parse functions
from      libParse import BEFORE
from      libParse import AFTER
from      libParse import INCL
from      libParse import EXCL

import libSelenium        # Selenium (chromedriver) specific functions


# # # # # # # # # # # # # #
# Manage Logs
try:
        os.system("del *.log")
except:
        libBot.writeLog(logFile, "There were no log files to remove.")

print("\n")
libBot.writeLog(logFile, "############################################")
libBot.writeLog(logFile, "# " + scriptName)
```

```
libBot.writeLog(logFile, "#############################################")
libBot.writeLog(logFile, "Log file: " + logFile)

# Load Selenium (get driver) and resize/reposition the browser window
driver = libSelenium.loadWebdriver(logFile, pathChromeDriver)
libSelenium.setWindowSize(logFile, driver, x=800, y=800)
libSelenium.setWindowPosition(logFile, driver, x=10, y=10)

##########################################################################
##########################################################################
## Start: PAYLOAD (This is where the work is performed.)
##

libBot.writeLog(logFile, "Delete any old CSV files")
os.system("del *.csv")

def initCSV():
        csv = ["", "", "", "", "", "", "",  "", ""]
        return csv

#------------------------------------
def writeCSV(logFile, fileName, array):
        header = '"DATE", "NAME_FIRST", "NAME_LAST", "STREET_1", "STREET_2", "CITY",
"STATE", "POSTAL_CODE", "GROUP"\n'

        # if file doesn't exist, write the header
        if not os.path.isfile(fileName):
                libBot.writeLog(logFile, "Creating new CSV file")
                libBot.writeFile(logFile, fileName, header)

        # write the array into the csv file
        csv = ""
        for data in array:
                csv = csv + '"'+data.strip()+'", '

        libBot.appendFile(logFile, fileName, csv+"\n")

#------------------------------------

##########################################################################
# Get first source

# Download the page
libBot.writeLog(logFile, "Getting the first source.")
domain = "https://mepso.com/"
path = "publishing/selenium_python/examples/parseAggregation/group1.php"
libBot.writeLog(logFile, "Getting: " + domain+path)
driver.get(domain+path)
libBot.randomWait(logFile, 2, 3)

# Separate the text to parse from everything else
tableHTML = driver.execute_script("return document.getElementById('orders').innerHTML;")
tableHTML = libParse.strReplace(" ", "", tableHTML)
```

121

```
ArrRows = libParse.parseArray(tableHTML, "<tr", "</tr>", EXCL)

for row in range(1, len(ArrRows)):
        thisRow = ArrRows[row]
        thisRow = libParse.strReplace("\n", "", thisRow)
        ArrCells        = libParse.parseArray(thisRow, "<td ", "</td>", INCL)

        csv = initCSV()
        csv[0]  = timeStart

        for cell in range(1, 8):
                csv[cell]       = libParse.stripTags(ArrCells[cell]).strip()

        # Go back and clean-up the address cell
        csv[3] = libParse.stripTags(ArrCells[3])
        csv[3] = libParse.strReplace("  ", "~", csv[3])
        csv[3] = libParse.strReplace("~", "", csv[3])

        # Add group
        csv[8]  = "Group 1"

        libBot.writeLog(logFile, "Writing line to CSV file")
        writeCSV(logFile, "test.csv", csv)

libBot.randomWait(logFile, 10, 11)

# endOf Get first source
#--------------------------------

########################################################################
# Get second source

# Download the page
libBot.writeLog(logFile, "Getting the second source.")
domain = "http://mepso.com/"
path = "publishing/selenium_python/examples/parseAggregation/group2.php"
libBot.writeLog(logFile, "Getting: " + domain+path)
driver.get(domain+path)
libBot.randomWait(logFile, 2, 3)

maxRows = 40
for row in range(2, maxRows):

        '''
        STARTof: Table XPATH                                            | Member |
Street | City | State | Postal Code |
        # First line in table                                          +--------
+--------+------+-------+------------+
        /html/body/table/tbody/tr[2]/td[1]        ------> |        |        |        |
|             |
        /html/body/table/tbody/tr[2]/td[2] --------------------^
        /html/body/table/tbody/tr[2]/td[3] ----------------------------^
        /html/body/table/tbody/tr[2]/td[3] ------------------------------------^
```

```
        /html/body/table/tbody/tr[2]/td[5]
------------------------------------------------^

        # Second line in table
        /html/body/table/tbody/tr[3]/td[1]
        /html/body/table/tbody/tr[3]/td[3]
        /html/body/table/tbody/tr[3]/td[2]...
        ENDof: Table XPATH


        Sample row (record):
        <tr><td  bgcolor='papayawhip'  ><a
                  href="javascript:void(0)"
                  title="Esme Jones"
                  >E. J</a></td><td  bgcolor='papayawhip'  >4147 76th Avenue</td><td
bgcolor='papayawhip'  >Stoke</td><td  bgcolor='papayawhip'  >OH</td><td align="right"
bgcolor='papayawhip'  >73940</td>
    </tr>


        '''


        try:
                # parse name from initials
                xpathTxt =  "/html/body/table/tbody/tr["+str(row)+"]/td[1]"
                temp = driver.find_element(By.XPATH, xpathTxt)
                nameHTML = temp.get_attribute("innerHTML")

                nameFirst = libParse.returnBetween(nameHTML, 'title="', '&', EXCL)
                nameLast = libParse.returnBetween(nameHTML, ' ', '"', EXCL)

                # Street (1 and 2)
                xpathTxt =  "/html/body/table/tbody/tr["+str(row)+"]/td[2]"
                street = driver.find_element(By.XPATH, xpathTxt).text
                if libParse.stristr(street, ","):
                        street1 = libParse.splitString(street, ",", BEFORE, EXCL)
                        street2 = libParse.splitString(street, ",", AFTER, EXCL)
                else:
                        street1 = libParse.stripTags(street).strip()
                        street2 = ""

                # city
                xpathTxt =  "/html/body/table/tbody/tr["+str(row)+"]/td[3]"
                city = driver.find_element(By.XPATH, xpathTxt).text

                # state
                xpathTxt =  "/html/body/table/tbody/tr["+str(row)+"]/td[4]"
                state = driver.find_element(By.XPATH, xpathTxt).text

                # postalCode
                xpathTxt =  "/html/body/table/tbody/tr["+str(row)+"]/td[5]"
                postalCode = driver.find_element(By.XPATH, xpathTxt).text

                # write to CSV file
```

```
                csv = initCSV()
                csv[0]  = timeStart
                csv[1]  = nameFirst
                csv[2]  = nameLast
                csv[3]  = street1
                csv[4]  = street2
                csv[5]  = city
                csv[6]  = state
                csv[7]  = postalCode.strip()
                csv[8]  = "Group 2"
                libBot.writeLog(logFile, "Writing line to CSV file")
                writeCSV(logFile, "test.csv", csv)
        except:
                print("We found the last row")
                break

libBot.randomWait(logFile, 10, 11)


# endOf Get second soruce
#--------------------------------
######################################################################
# Get third source

# Download the page
libBot.writeLog(logFile, "Getting the third source.")
domain = "http://mepso.com/"
path = "publishing/selenium_python/examples/parseAggregation/group3.php"
libBot.writeLog(logFile, "Getting: " + domain+path)
driver.get(domain+path)
libBot.randomWait(logFile, 2, 3)


# Separate the text to parse from everything else
html = libBot.getWebpageContents(logFile, driver) + "</tag>"
html = libParse.strReplace("Name:", "</tag><tag>", html)

ArrOrders = libParse.parseArray(html, "<tag>", "</tag>", EXCL)

for row in range(0, len(ArrOrders)):

        name = libParse.splitString(ArrOrders[row], "Street:", BEFORE, EXCL)
        street = libParse.returnBetween(ArrOrders[row], "Street:", "\n", EXCL)

        if libParse.stristr(ArrOrders[row], "Address:"):
                street2 = libParse.returnBetween(ArrOrders[row], "Address:", "City/State:",
EXCL)
        else:
                street2 = ""

        cityStateZip = libParse.splitString(ArrOrders[row], "State:", AFTER, EXCL)
        stateZip = libParse.returnBetween(cityStateZip, ",", "\n", EXCL).strip()

        city  = libParse.splitString(cityStateZip, ",", BEFORE, EXCL)
        state = libParse.splitString(stateZip, " ", BEFORE, EXCL)
```

124

```
        zipCode = libParse.splitString(stateZip, " ", AFTER, EXCL)

        csv = ["", "", "", "", "", "", "", "", ""]
        csv[0]  = timeStart
        csv[1]  = libParse.splitString(name, " ", BEFORE, EXCL).strip()
        csv[2]  = libParse.splitString(name, " ", AFTER, EXCL).strip()
        csv[3]  = street.strip()
        csv[4]  = street2.strip()

        csv[5]  = city
        csv[6]  = state
        csv[7]  = zipCode
        csv[8]  = "Group 3"
        libBot.writeLog(logFile, "Writing line to CSV file")
        writeCSV(logFile, "test.csv", csv)

        # endOf Get third soruce
        #---------------------------------

libBot.randomWait(logFile, 10, 13)

# ENDOF Payload
########################################################################
########################################################################

# # # # # # # # # # # # # #
# Close gracefully
libBot.closeBot(logFile, driver, "Exiting normally: "+scriptName)
########################################################################
```

Script 9.15, parseAggregate.py in its entirety

## CHAPTER 10

PROJ 07: REGRESSION TESTS

One of the more common uses for Selenium is for testing websites. And one of the more common tests is a Regression Test.

Regression tests are a type of software testing that is performed to ensure that changes or updates made to a software application do not unintentionally introduce new bugs or issues. It is like double-checking that previously working features continue to function correctly after modifications have been made, and that the codebase hasn't regressed to a prior state..

To better explain, imagine a familiar scenario: Let's say you have a favorite app on your phone that you use every day. One day, the app gets updated with new features and improvements. Regression tests would be similar to you checking that all the existing functionalities you rely on, like logging in, browsing content, or sending messages, still work as expected after the update.

The purpose of regression tests is to catch any unexpected issues that may have been introduced during the software development process or as a result of changes in other parts of the software. By validating the core functionalities of the software through regression tests, developers can have more confidence in the stability and reliability of the application.

Watch the associated video on YouTube

There is a supplemental video on YouTube where you can watch demonstration of this bot as well as a narrated code walk-through. Go to www.mepso.com and click on the link for this book on the home page. There you'll find links to videos and library code downloads.

Figure 10.1, Link to chapter video

Exploring the target website

The website within our target is that of a fictitious company named Pacific Heights Competitive Intelligence, as shown in Figure 10.2.

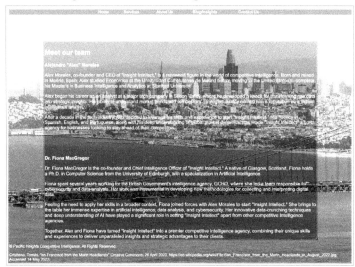

Figure 10.2, The home page of the target website for our regression test

The website is simple, reminiscent of mid-90's NASA web pages. But the owners of the business are aware of this and are anticipating that the site will grow and improve as their business grows.

The website currently has five pages:

1. A home page,

2. A page that describes the intelligence services they provide,

3. An "about us" page,

4. A blog page, and

5. A simple contact page.

The regression test

The owners of the company are forward thinking, so in addition to verifying that all of the expected functions to function, they also want to watch the website mature and improve.

So, they commissioned a piece of software that:

- Runs at least once a day,

- For each test, creates a single log file for each page that records:

  ○ The Page URL,

  ○ The directory where the logs go,

  ○ The time it takes to download the web page,

  ○ The metadata keywords,

  ○ The number of times each of the keywords is used on the page.

- Places a screen shot of the web page in the page's test directory.

Let's explore how we accomplish that list of tasks.

Code walk-through

As with the other examples that use the framework from Project 2, this code walk-through will be limited to the script's payload. We will also allow the framework to gracefully exit when the program completes.

The payload starts by defining a header that is used to format a CSV file where the regression test data is stored.

Once the header is defined, the bot downloads the first page it tests. Once the page is downloaded, the bot harvests all the links.

These links will create a list of pages that is included in the regression test session, but only if they are onsite links, as shown in Script 10.1.

```
########################################################################
## Start: PAYLOAD (This is where the work is performed.)
##
ARRcsvHeader = ["TIMESTAMP", "URL", "PATH", "LOAD_TIME", "TITLE", "SIZE", "KEYWORDS",
"KEYWORD_OCCURRENCE"]

# Get the initial web page
seedURL ="http://www.mepso.com/publishing/selenium_python/examples/regression/"
libBot.writeLog(logFile, "Fetching the seed url")
libBot.writeLog(logFile, seedURL)
driver.get(seedURL)
libBot.randomWait(logFile, 3, 5)

# Harvest all the links from the initial page
libBot.writeLog(logFile, "gathering page links from seed page")
html = libBot.getWebpageContents(logFile, driver)
ARRlinks = libParse.parse_array(html, 'href="', '"')

# Validate that these are onsite links
libBot.writeLog(logFile, "Verify that these are all on-site links")
ARRvalidLinks = []
for href in ARRlinks:
    print(href)
    if libParse.stristr(href, "http"):
        if(libParse.stristr, href, "mepso.com"):
                ARRvalidLinks.append(str(href))
    else:
        ARRvalidLinks.append(str(href))
```

Script 10.1, Regression test initialization and link collection

Once the bot has a list of validated URLs, it iterates through the list and performs an identical procedure for each page it tests.

The first thing that is done is the definition, and creation of the test file structure, if it doesn't already exist, as shown in Script 10.2.

```
libBot.writeLog(logFile, "Loop through the onsite links to test each URL")
for href in ARRvalidLinks:

        # Initialize the ARRcsv (where we collect the data we'll write ito the CSV file)
        ARRcsv = []
        ARRcsv.append(timeStart)

        absoluteURL = libBot.getAbsoluteAddress(logFile, driver, href)
```

```
ARRcsv.append(absoluteURL)

# get root name of script so we can make test directories for each page
index = absoluteURL.rfind("//")
subBefore, docName = libParse.splitStringAtIndex(absoluteURL, index+2)
docName = libParse.strReplace(".", "_", docName)

index = docName.rfind("/")
subBefore, pageName = libParse.splitStringAtIndex(absoluteURL, index+2)

docName = libParse.strReplace("/", "_", docName)
ARRcsv.append(docName)

# If the test directory doesn't exist, make it
testDirectory = "testlogs/"+docName
if os.path.exists(testDirectory) and os.path.isdir(testDirectory):
        libBot.writeLog(logFile, "The directory:"+testDirectory+" exists")
else:
        libBot.writeLog(logFile, "Creating directory:"+testDirectory)
        os.mkdir(testDirectory)

# Create a log file, if one isn't already crated
csvPath = "testlogs/"+docName+"/logs.csv"
if os.path.exists(csvPath):
        libBot.writeLog(logFile, csvPath+" exists")
else:
        libBot.writeLog(logFile, "Creating log.csv file")
        libBot.writeCSV(logFile, csvPath, ARRcsvHeader)
```

Script 10.2, defining and creating the test file structure

Once the file structure is ensured, the bot proceeds to measure and record website parametrics that were defined in the ARRcsvHeader, including a timestamp, identification of the page in test, load times, links, and a set of parametrics related to keywords and the frequency of their use, as shown in Script 10.3.

```
libBot.writeLog(logFile, "Load page and record load times")
timeA = time.time()
driver.get(absoluteURL)
timeB = time.time()
ARRcsv.append(str(timeB-timeA))

libBot.randomWait(logFile, 3, 5)


title = libParse.parsePageTitle(logFile, driver)
ARRcsv.append(title)

head = libParse.parsePageHead(logFile, driver)

ARRlinks = libParse.parse_array(html, 'href="', '"')
```

```
ARRvalidLinks = []
for href in ARRlinks:
        absoluteURL = libBot.getAbsoluteAddress(logFile, driver, href)
        if(libParse.stristr, href, "mepso.com"):
                ARRvalidLinks.append(str(absoluteURL))

html = libBot.getWebpageContents(logFile, driver)
ARRcsv.append(len(html))

ARRkeyWords=libParse.parsePageKeywords(logFile, driver)

keywordString =""
for keyword in ARRkeyWords:
        keywordString = keywordString + keyword + "\n"

ARRcsv.append(keywordString)

keywordString =""
for keyword in ARRkeyWords:
        countKeyword = html.count(keyword)
        keywordString = keywordString + str(countKeyword) + "\n"
        libBot.writeLog(logFile, keyword + " was found " + str(countKeyword) + "
times.")
```

Script 10.3, Recording parametric data

The one last metric, that is recorded is a screen shot of the web page under test. This snapshot is performed with the code below in Script 10.4.

```
driver.save_screenshot(testDirectory + "/img_" + timeStart + ".png")
```

Script 10.4, Creating a screen shot of a web page

Areas for growth

This is perhaps the world's simplest regression test. Can you think of ways to improve it? Here's a short list to get you started.

1. Setting the test up to run as a scheduled task or cron job,

2. Checking for spelling and linkage errors,

3. If there's authentication, verify that former employees can't log into the site, and

4. A call to action when it finds an error.

Script: regression.py

```
#######################################################################
scriptName = "regression" + ".py"
#--------------------------
# # # # # # # # # # # # # #
# Configuration
import   sys
import   os
import   time

from     datetime          import datetime
from     random            import randint

import   selenium
from      selenium.webdriver.common.by import By
from      selenium.webdriver.common.keys import Keys

# # # # # # # # # # # # # # #
# Record the start time
start_time = time.time()
timeStart = datetime.today().strftime('%Y%m%d_%H%M%S')

# # # # # # # # # # # # # # # #
# Establish paths and import libraries
#
sys.path.insert(0, "../../libs")          # Import local libraries
from     libPaths          import logFile
from     libPaths          import pathChromeDriver
from     libPaths          import pathRoot

import   libBot             # Useful bot functions

import   libParse # Parse functions
from      libParse import BEFORE
from      libParse import AFTER
from      libParse import INCL
from      libParse import EXCL

import libSelenium          # Selenium (chromedriver) specific functions


# # # # # # # # # # # # # # #
# Manage Logs
try:
        os.system("del *.log")
except:
        libBot.writeLog(logFile, "There were no log files to remove.")

print("\n")
libBot.writeLog(logFile, "#############################################")
libBot.writeLog(logFile, "# " + scriptName)
libBot.writeLog(logFile, "#############################################")
```

```
libBot.writeLog(logFile, "Log file: " + logFile)

# Load Selenium (get driver) and resize/reposition the browser window
driver = libSelenium.loadWebdriver(logFile, pathChromeDriver)
libSelenium.setWindowSize(logFile, driver, x=800, y=800)
libSelenium.setWindowPosition(logFile, driver, x=10, y=10)

#########################################################################
#########################################################################
## Start: PAYLOAD (This is where the work is performed.)

ARRcsvHeader = ["TIMESTAMP", "URL", "PATH", "LOAD_TIME", "TITLE", "SIZE", "KEYWORDS",
"KEYWORD_OCCURRENCE"]

seedURL ="http://www.mepso.com/publishing/selenium_python/examples/regression/"
libBot.writeLog(logFile, "Fetching the seed url")
libBot.writeLog(logFile, seedURL)

try:
        driver.get(seedURL)
        libBot.randomWait(logFile, 3, 5)

        ###########################################
        # Get all the links from the home page
        libBot.writeLog(logFile, "gathering page links from seed page")
        html = libBot.getWebpageContents(logFile, driver)
        ARRlinks = libParse.parseArray(html, 'href="', '"', EXCL)

        ###########################################
        # Gather link of all onsite links
        libBot.writeLog(logFile, "Verify that these are all on-site links")
        ARRvalidLinks = []
        for href in ARRlinks:
                libBot.writeLog(logFile, "Testing link: "+href)
                absoluteURL = libBot.getAbsoluteAddress(logFile, driver, href)
                if(libParse.stristr, href, "mepso.com"):
                        libBot.writeLog(logFile, "Onsite")
                        ARRvalidLinks.append(str(href))            # Add to valid link
array
                else:
                        libBot.writeLog(logFile, "Offsite")

        ###########################################
        # Conduct tests on each valid page
        libBot.writeLog(logFile, "Loop through the onsite links to test each URL")
        for href in ARRvalidLinks:

                libBot.writeLog(logFile, "### START of Page Loop ###")

                ###########################################
                # Initialize the ARRcsv (where we collect the data we'll write ito the CSV
file)
                ARRcsv = []
```

```
        ARRcsv.append(timeStart)                # ARRcsv[0]

        ############################################
        # Get absolute URL
        absoluteURL = libBot.getAbsoluteAddress(logFile, driver, href)
        ARRcsv.append(absoluteURL)                # ARRcsv[1]

        ############################################
        # get root name of script so we can make test directories for each page
        index = absoluteURL.rfind("//")
        subBefore, docName = libParse.splitStringAtIndex(absoluteURL, index+2)
        docName = libParse.strReplace(".", "_", docName)

        index = docName.rfind("/")
        subBefore, pageName = libParse.splitStringAtIndex(absoluteURL, index+2)

        docName = libParse.strReplace("/", "_", docName)
        ARRcsv.append(docName)                    # ARRcsv[2]

        ############################################
        # If the test directory doesn't exist, make it
        testDirectory = "testlogs/"+docName
        if os.path.exists(testDirectory) and os.path.isdir(testDirectory):
                libBot.writeLog(logFile, "The directory:"+testDirectory+" exists")
        else:
                libBot.writeLog(logFile, "Creating directory:"+testDirectory)
                os.mkdir(testDirectory)

        ############################################
        # Create a log file, if one isn't already crated
        csvPath = "testlogs/"+docName+"/logs.csv"
        if os.path.exists(csvPath):
                libBot.writeLog(logFile, csvPath+" exists")
        else:
                libBot.writeLog(logFile, "Creating log.csv file")
                libBot.writeCSV(logFile, csvPath, ARRcsvHeader)

        ############################################
        # Record load times
        libBot.writeLog(logFile, "Load page and record load times")
        timeA = time.time()
        driver.get(absoluteURL)
        timeB = time.time()
        ARRcsv.append(str(timeB-timeA))           # ARRcsv[3]

        libBot.randomWait(logFile, 3, 5)

        ############################################
        # Record page title
        title = libParse.parsePageTitle(logFile, driver)
        ARRcsv.append(title)                      # ARRcsv[4]

        ############################################
```

```
                # Record page length( butes)
                html = libBot.getWebpageContents(logFile, driver)
                ARRcsv.append(len(html))

                ###########################################
                # Record keywords
                ARRkeyWords=libParse.parsePageKeywords(logFile, driver)

                keywordString =""
                for keyword in ARRkeyWords:
                        keywordString = keywordString + keyword + "\n"

                ARRcsv.append(keywordString)        # ARRcsv[5]

                ###########################################
                # Record keyword Occurrence
                keywordOccurrenceString =""
                for keyword in ARRkeyWords:
                        countKeyword = html.count(keyword)
                        keywordOccurrenceString = keywordOccurrenceString +
str(countKeyword) + "\n"
                        libBot.writeLog(logFile, keyword + " was found " +
str(countKeyword) + " times.")

                ARRcsv.append(keywordOccurrenceString)             # ARRcsv[6]

                ###########################################
                # Write new line of data to the CSV file in this page's directory
                libBot.writeCSV(logFile, csvPath, ARRcsv)

                ###########################################
                # screen capture of this page  in this page's directory
                libBot.writeLog(logFile, testDirectory + "/img_" + timeStart + ".png")

                driver.save_screenshot(testDirectory + "/img_" + timeStart + ".png")

                libBot.writeLog(logFile, "### END of Page Loop ###")

except:
        libBot.writeLog(logFile, "Failed to download seedURL "+seedURL)


# ENDOF Payload
######################################################################
######################################################################

# # # # # # # # # # # # # # #
# Close gracefully
libBot.closeBot(logFile, driver, "Exiting normally: "+scriptName)
######################################################################
```

136

## CHAPTER 11

PROJ 08: SOLVING CAPTCHAS

CAPTCHAs, or Completely Automated Public Test to tell Computers and Humans Apart, are devices that web developers use to discourage bot traffic. They've been around nearly as long as the Internet, and have frustrated users with their cryptic, hard-to-read solutions for decades. While they are frequently the wrath of Interface and Usability Engineers as well as ADA advocates, CAPTCHAs have been successful at blocking traffic—much of it from bots.

In reality, CAPTCHAs are little more than speed bumps for well equipped bots.

Shown below, in Figure 11.1, is a typical CAPTCHA[7]. This is the type of CAPTCHA that we will be solving—where the contents of an image must be typed into a text box, but the techniques used here should transfer well to other types of CAPTCHAs as well.

Figure 11.1, CAPTCHA example (not the actual one we'll be solving)

These devices take many forms. Some CAPTCHAs may ask you to type text that is embedded into an image. Another might display a matrix of city views and request that the viewer click on all the boxes that contain streetlights. But they all have the same

---

7 *BotDetect Captcha Generator*. BotDetect CAPTCHA Generator. (n.d.). https://captcha.com/

goal, to stop bots and allow human traffic through, with a minimal amount of interference.

Legitimate reasons for defeating CAPTCHAs

Throughout this book, you will read that it's important to develop bots that respect sources—if for no other reason, than to help extend the life of the project and to protect trade secrets. After all, if your bot's sources dry-up because of misbehavior, your bot won't be worth much. Beyond that, there should be a level of professionalism that demands that one doesn't use bots in ways that are unfriendly to the community at large.

That being said, there are some legitimate reasons to develop bots that can solve/defeat[8] CAPTCHAs.

You're developing bots that test websites

If you're testing websites—either for your organization or for those of clients, you will need to test every CAPTCHAs used on those pages. And the test should include at least one case where the CAPTCHA is solved, and at least one instance where the CAPTCHA attempt fails.

You're accessing data you paid to accessed

Often, bots will need to harvest data from paid sources. Sometimes these sources use CAPTCHAs. If you're bot accesses a paid source, you will likely need to solve a CAPTCHA.

You've been throttled

I've seen websites use CAPTCHAs well into sessions for the purpose of *throttling,* or slowing down user of websites. This sometimes happens when one accesses data too quickly, or is making an excessive number of queries.

---

8   Depending on which political side you favor.

When you encounter a throttle, not only do you need to equip your bot with the ability to solve the CAPTCHA, but it is also a sign to SLOW DOWN. It's always best to take the hint and keep a source happy.

This may not be a complete list. I'm sure that other situations also exist.

Watch the associated video on YouTube

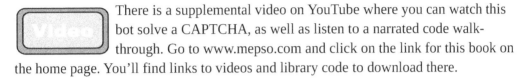

There is a supplemental video on YouTube where you can watch this bot solve a CAPTCHA, as well as listen to a narrated code walk-through. Go to www.mepso.com and click on the link for this book on the home page. You'll find links to videos and library code to download there.

Figure 11.2, Link to chapter video

CAPTCHAs are a form of authentication

When a bot encounters a CAPTCHA, the application is asking if the viewer is human. This is a little different than asking if someone is who they specifically say they are, but both are forms of authentication.

Authentication is usually accomplished with one (or more) of the following techniques.

Test what the viewer knows

This refers to some knowledge-based information that only the authorized user should possess such as: Passwords, PINs, or Answers to personal security questions.

Test what the viewer has

Authorized users may have been given something that can uniquely identify them. This item may be anything from physical object like a key or a digital token that serves as proof of identity.

Test what the viewer is

This authentication involves characteristics unique to an individual, including: Fingerprints, Iris scans, Voice recognition, Facial recognition, or a Specific Skill.

In the case of CAPTCHAs, authentication has been based on performing a task that is easy for humans, but more difficult for computers. So, CAPTCHAs test authenticity by testing what the viewer is—a human that has the skills to interpret a challenge.

CAPTCHA solving services

I've had great success using CAPTCHA solving services for many years. These services are much easier to use than home-spun solutions. And, he ones I've used were cheap (much less than a penny per solution) and had an accuracy rate of around 97%.

This project employs one such CAPTCHA solving service. These services can be found with a simple Google search. I reached out to one of the services that I've used in the past, with the intent to interview them. To no one's surprise, none of them took me up on my offer. These services are easy to find and are available to solve any and all types of CAPTCHAs.

The CAPTCHA solving industry

To my surprise—and to the surprise of most, there is an entire ecosystem dedicated to solving CAPTCHAs for bots[9]. This industry involves individuals or organizations that offer services to solve CAPTCHAs on behalf of others. Typically these services are used by automated systems, like ours, where there's a need to bypass CAPTCHA-protected systems.

The CAPTCHA solving industry operates through a combination of human solvers, *OCR* or Optical Character Readers, and automated algorithms. Today, human solvers are still a big part of the industry.

The story that I've been told, is that people in developing countries answer ads for jobs that "Pay Cash Daily" or "Solve Puzzles for Cash". Once hired, employees load a special website on their computer or phone where they physically solve the CAPTCHA images

---

9   Woods, D. (2021, May 14). *I was a human CAPTCHA SOLVER.* F5 Labs. https://www.f5.com/labs/articles/cisotociso/i-was-a-human-captcha-solver

that are sent to them. I've been told—but have no proof, that three solution for the same problem are compared. If two agree on the answer, then that becomes the answer.

I've been told that people are able to send themselves through college this way. If this is true, they're working a lot because it cost much less than $0.01 to solve a CAPTCHA through a service. And that includes the agency fee.

And here's the ugly side

Like many aspects of botDev, the CAPTCHA solving industry offers convenience and efficiency for those of us, who are seeking to automate tasks or bypass CAPTCHAs for legitimate commercial purposes. Conversely, finding automated ways to solve CAPTCHAs also raises ethical concerns. The use of CAPTCHA solvers can enable malicious activities, such as spamming, credential stuffing, or other forms of automated abuse. Furthermore, CAPTCHA solvers undermine the security measures put in place to protect online systems from automated attacks.

Other uses for CAPTCHAs

At one point, Google was sourcing CAPTCHA text from turn-of-the-century newspapers and books. As people solved these CAPTCHAs, they were simultaneously digitizing old documents. A win-win!

Unfortunately, hackers soon realized that these CAPTCHA algorithms assumed that when a number of people had the same solution for the same image, that that solution became the correct digital translation for that word. Hackers then correctly assumed that if enough people said "dog" when the CAPTCHA word was "cat", the solution for "cat" would eventually become "dog".

The future of CAPTCHAs

In response to the arms race between CAPTCHA developers and solvers, CAPTCHA systems have evolved to become more complex and challenging. Newer technologies, such as reCAPTCHA by Google, employ advanced techniques like image recognition, behavioral analysis, and risk scoring to differentiate between humans and bots. These advancements aim to make automated CAPTCHA solving more difficult and deter the use of CAPTCHA-solving services.

The dichotomy of all of these advances is that CAPTCHAs still need to be predictably, and automatically, solvable or they cannot be tested.

That's enough about CAPTCHAs. Let's get on to the project.

The CAPTCHA

The page where our project's CAPCHA challenge exists is shown below in Figure 11.3.

Figure 11.3, The CAPTCHA to be solved

Please note that the context for this CAPTCHA page is educational and not functional. In other words, it's not a real CAPTCHA, but it works fine for our purposes and created specifically for this use.

On this page you'll find a dynamically created image that contains the letters that complete the CAPTCHA solution. To solve the challenge, our bot needs to interpret and transfer those characters to the text box and submit the solution. The theory is that one would have to be human to complete such a feat. But in this project, we'll convince a machine that our bot isn't a machine.

The CAPTCHA solving service

Shown below is the CAPTCHA solution provider we'll be using.

 I am certain that people could hack either the CAPTCHA solver or the CAPCHA test we're using. Please don't try to hack either of these web pages. It's not worth the effort.

I'll be the first to point out that this is not a real CAPTCHA solver as described earlier. I hate to break this to you, but there are no live people on the other side of this website interpreting the images or OCR readers. This services is actually a trick for the purposes of this project.

Our CAPCHA solver is shown in Figure 11.4.

Figure 11.4, the API of the CAPTCHA solver.

The CAPTCHA solvers I've used look and perform very much like the one above. In the solutions I've used, there is always a human usable form, like the one in the figure above, as well as a more formalize API.

In our case, we will use Selenium to open the CAPTCHA to be solved in one browser tab, then open a second browser tab to house the solver. The image, containing the

CAPTCHA code will be downloaded from the CAPTCHA page by our bot. That image is then uploaded to the solver.

Once the CAPCHA image is uploaded, it is validated and a solution is provided, as shown in the figure on the next page.

Figure 11.5, The CAPTCHA solver and a solution

In our case, the solution is performed through trickery and imagination. But in real world examples, CAPTCHAs are solve through a combination of human puzzle solvers and optical recognition software.

In our case, the answer is easily parsed, when we look at the source code for the solution, as seen below.

```
<h1>Your Friendly CAPTCHA Solver<sup>*</sup></h1>

<form action="index.php" method="POST" enctype="multipart/form-data">

<input type="file" name="fileToUpload" id="fileToUpload">

<input type="submit" value="Upload File" name="submit">

</form>

ANSWER: <answer>RMLI</answer>
```

Figure 11.6, A detail of the solved CAPTCHA

Fortunately, the answer is easy to parse, as it is contained in a nice pair of `<answer>` `</answer>` tags, as shown. Notice that the answer "RMLI" is correct.

Let's look at the bots code. And don't forget, there's a video of a bot demo and code walk-through on YouTube.

Code walk-through

Step one is to load the target web page, as shown below in Script 11.1.

```
#########################################################################
#########################################################################
## Start: PAYLOAD (This is where the work is performed.)
##
libBot.writeLog(logFile, "Get the initial captcha web page")
driver.get("http://mepso.com/publishing/selenium_python/examples/captchas/")
driver.set_window_size(900, 875)
libBot.randomWait(logFile, 2, 3)


###########################################
# Download the CAPTCHA image file

libBot.writeLog(logFile, "Get the url of the first image")
image_element = driver.find_element(By.XPATH,'/html/body/table/tbody/tr[1]/td/img')
image_url = image_element.get_attribute('src')

libBot.writeLog(logFile, "Download the image file")
response = requests.get(image_url)
image_file_path = pathRoot + 'image.png'
with open(image_file_path, 'wb') as file:
    file.write(response.content)
```

Script 11.1, Downloading the CAPTCHA image to be solved

Once the image is had, it needs to be uploaded to our CAPTCHA solving service. The bot chooses to keep the prior webpage (with the CAPTCHA) available, so it opens a new browser tab with Selenium for the service that solves the CAPTCHA, as shown on the next page.

```
##########################################
# Upload image to CAPTCHA Solver and get solution
libBot.writeLog(logFile, "Open, and move to, new browser tab")
window_ORG = driver.current_window_handle          # Record handle of first tab
driver.execute_script("window.open('');")           # Open new browser tab
driver.switch_to.window(driver.window_handles[1])   # Move to new browser tab
window_ALT = driver.current_window_handle           # Record handle of second tab
libBot.randomWait(logFile, 4, 5)

libBot.writeLog(logFile, "Load the captcha solver into new tab")
driver.get("http://mepso.com/publishing/selenium_python/examples/captchaSolver/")
libBot.randomWait(logFile, 2, 3)
```

Script 11.2, Opening a new browser tab for the CAPTCHA solver web page

The API on the CAPTCHA solver is really easy to use of you have the facility to use it as a web page, and with Selenium we do. So it's as easy as location the file upload field's name and sending the text string containing the image file path. Then its just a simple matter of clicking on the submit button, as shown below.

```
libBot.writeLog(logFile, "Enter image name into form")
driver.find_element(By.NAME, "fileToUpload").send_keys(image_file_path)
libBot.randomWait(logFile, 2, 3)

libBot.writeLog(logFile, "Submit form")
driver.find_element(By.NAME, "submit").click()
libBot.randomWait(logFile, 4, 5)
```

Script 11.3, uploading the CAPTCHA image

The CAPTCHA solver provides a solution to the CAPTCHA *(i.e., the decoding the of text in the CAPTCHA image)* and displays the solution on the next page refresh. For parsing ease, the solution is bracketed by <answer> </answer> tags.

```
##########################################
# Get the solved CAPTCHA answer and submit to the CAPTCHA
libBot.writeLog(logFile, "Getting copy of solution")
html = libBot.getWebpageContents(logFile, driver)
answer = libParse.returnBetween(html, "<answer>", "</answer>")
libBot.writeLog(logFile, "THE APTCHA SOLUTION IS: " + answer)

libBot.writeLog(logFile, "Go back to original (CAPTCHA) window")
driver.switch_to.window(window_ORG)
libBot.randomWait(logFile, 1, 2)
libBot.writeLog(logFile, "Submit answer")
driver.find_element(By.NAME, "code").send_keys(answer)
libBot.randomWait(logFile, 1, 2)
driver.find_element(By.NAME, "code").send_keys(Keys.ENTER)
```

```
libBot.randomWait(logFile, 4, 5)
html = libBot.getWebpageContents(logFile, driver)
print(html)
# ENDOF PAYLOAD
########################################################################
########################################################################
```

Script 11.4, Parsing the CAPTCHA solution

Script: captchaSolver.py

```
###################################################################
scriptName = "captchaSolver" + ".py"
#---------------------------
# # # # # # # # # # # # # #
# Configuration
import    sys
import    os
import    time
import    urllib            # NOTE This was added just for this project…!

from      datetime          import datetime
from      random            import randint

import    selenium
from       selenium.webdriver.common.by import By
from       selenium.webdriver.common.keys import Keys


# # # # # # # # # # # # # # #
# Record the start time
start_time = time.time()
timeStart = datetime.today().strftime('%Y%m%d_%H%M%S')


# # # # # # # # # # # # # # #
# Establish paths and import libraries
#
sys.path.insert(0, "../../libs")        # Import local libraries
from      libPaths          import logFile
from      libPaths          import pathChromeDriver
from      libPaths          import pathRoot

import    libBot            # Useful bot functions

import    libParse # Parse functions
from      libParse import BEFORE
from      libParse import AFTER
from      libParse import INCL
from      libParse import EXCL

import libSelenium          # Selenium (chromedriver) specific functions



# # # # # # # # # # # # # # #
# Manage Logs
try:
        os.system("del *.log")
except:
        libBot.writeLog(logFile, "There were no log files to remove.")

print("\n")
libBot.writeLog(logFile, "###########################################")
libBot.writeLog(logFile, "# " + scriptName)
```

```
libBot.writeLog(logFile, "##########################################")
libBot.writeLog(logFile, "Log file: " + logFile)

# Load Selenium (get driver) and resize/reposition the browser window
driver = libSelenium.loadWebdriver(logFile, pathChromeDriver)
libSelenium.setWindowSize(logFile, driver, x=800, y=800)
libSelenium.setWindowPosition(logFile, driver, x=10, y=10)

########################################################################
########################################################################
## Start: PAYLOAD (This is where the work is performed.)
##
libBot.writeLog(logFile, "Get the initial captcha web page")
driver.get("http://mepso.com/publishing/selenium_python/examples/captchas/")
libBot.randomWait(logFile, 2, 3)

##########################################
# Download the CAPTCHA image file
libBot.writeLog(logFile, "Get the url of the first image")
image_element = driver.find_element(By.NAME, 'captchaImg')
image_url = image_element.get_attribute('src')
libBot.writeLog(logFile, "The 1st image is at:"+image_url)

libBot.writeLog(logFile, "Download the image file")
urllib.request.urlretrieve(image_url, "captcha.png")

libBot.randomWait(logFile, 10, 15)

##########################################
# Upload image to CAPTCHA Solver and get solution
libBot.writeLog(logFile, "Open, and move to, new browser tab")
window_ORG = driver.current_window_handle
driver.execute_script("window.open('');")
driver.switch_to.window(driver.window_handles[1])
window_ALT = driver.current_window_handle
libBot.randomWait(logFile, 4, 5)

libBot.writeLog(logFile, "Load the captcha solver into new tab")
driver.get("http://mepso.com/publishing/selenium_python/examples/captchaSolver/")
libBot.randomWait(logFile, 2, 3)

libBot.writeLog(logFile, "Enter image name into form")
driver.find_element(By.NAME,
"fileToUpload").send_keys("C:/Users/Administrator/Desktop/bots/selenium_python/examples/
captcha/captcha.png")
libBot.randomWait(logFile, 7, 8)

libBot.writeLog(logFile, "Submit form")
driver.find_element(By.NAME, "submit").click()
libBot.randomWait(logFile, 20, 25)

##########################################
# Get the solved CAPTCHA answer and submit to the CAPTCHA
```

```
libBot.writeLog(logFile, "Getting copy of solution")
html = libBot.getWebpageContents(logFile, driver)
answer = libParse.returnBetween(html, "<answer>", "</answer>", EXCL)
libBot.writeLog(logFile, "THE CAPTCHA SOLUTION IS: " +  answer)

libBot.writeLog(logFile, "Go back to original (CAPTCHA) window")
driver.switch_to.window(window_ORG)
libBot.randomWait(logFile, 1, 2)
libBot.writeLog(logFile, "Submit answer")
driver.find_element(By.NAME, "code").send_keys(answer)
libBot.randomWait(logFile, 1, 2)
driver.find_element(By.NAME, "code").send_keys(Keys.ENTER)

libBot.randomWait(logFile, 4, 5)
html = libBot.getWebpageContents(logFile, driver)

print(html)
libBot.randomWait(logFile, 10, 12)


# ENDOF Payload
########################################################################
########################################################################


# # # # # # # # # # # # # #
# Close gracefully
libBot.closeBot(logFile, driver, "Exiting normally: "+scriptName)
########################################################################
```

Script 11.6, The full script of captchaSolver.py

## CHAPTER 12

PROJ 09: BOTS THAT PLAY GAMES

This chapter challenges the reader to develop a bot that autonomously plays a game of Tic-Tac-Toe against another computer. Your mission is to: Write a bot that autonomously plays Tic-Tac-Toe with a computer opponent.

Another aspect of this project is that it produces really nice logs as the bot runs. We'll use this feature again in the next project where we'll explore *Selenium's "headless mode"*, or it's ability to execute the bot, blindly, without the use of a browser.

The part about the logs has become something of a joke with me, because I have become obsessive about logging, as I've learned it's importance.

Watch the supplemental video on YouTube

There is a video on YouTube where you can watch demonstration of this bot as well as get a narrated code walk-through. Go to www.mepso.com and click on the link for this book on the home page. You'll find links to videos and some code you can download there as well.

Figure 12.1, Link to chapter video

Sizing-up our opponent

The chosen opponent is the JavaScript-Tic-Tac-Toe-Project. This project was selected because the project is entirely written in HTML, CSS, and JavaScript, without any server interaction after the initial download.

This means that content is changed by the client, in JavaScript, without successive page reflows. Since the content is 100% active, so you won't see any of the players' moves by examining the page source.

I was also looking for an open source project that I could download and manage on my own servers without licensing issues. The JavaScript-Tic-Tac-Toe-Project is an Open Source project. You're free to download a copy for yourself at their GitHub page.

 Go ahead and check their project out. But before you start to practice writing and debugging your bot code, please use the copy of the game on mepso.com. They really don't need your "test" traffic.

They also claim that JavaScript-Tic-Tac-Toe-Project can't be beat. I don't know about that, but I'm also not ready to boast about how well our bot plays the game. But I think we're all up for the challenge.

The basic board layout of out opponent is depicted in Figure 12.2, below.

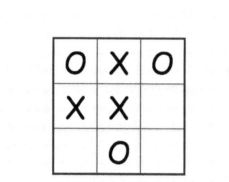

Figure: 12.2, The JavaScript Tic-Tac-Toe Project

You can find a copy of the application shown in Figure 12.2 at the Mepso Media website, as shown in Script 12.1.

```
https://www.mepso.com/seleniumPython/examples/tictaktoe/
```

Script 12.1 Location of target website

Rules for play (requirements)

This games-playing bot has few requirements, other than to play to win. But here is a short list of things to consider before our build:

1. Your bot always starts the game,

2. Your bot must detect if it is playing "O" or "X",

3. Your first move must be a random choice,

4. Your bot should attempt to play like a human, with adequate random delays.

5. Your bot should play declare the winner.

6. Your project should be based on the framework.py script shown earlier, with proper logging and library use. Logging will prove to be important…!

Examining the target (game play)

When the game loads, the board is blank and waiting for our bot to make the first move.

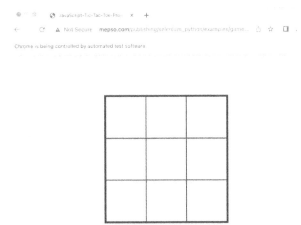

Figure: 12.3 Start of game

The game play is pretty straight forward. The challenger always starts, and is expected to click on the square that represents his or her opening move of choice. The game responds by planting an "O" in the square (if it's a legal move). The game then responds with it's own move—an "X" placed almost immediately, and quite strategically.

The game continues, turn after turn, until one opponent occupies three squares in a row, or all squares are occupied.

Defining the target's attributes

Before we begin on a bot that can play tic tac toe, we need to abstract the target. And by abstraction, I'm referring to determining how we are going to identify things, and how we will agree to operate on those things.

Here's what I came up with.

I first abstract the game board into a three by three table that corresponds to the game board. For each of those table cells, I assign an ID that corresponds to its position, as shown below in Script 12.2. So, using this system, the center square on the game board has an ID of 4. We'll refer to the table cells as "squares".

```
############################################################################
## Start: PAYLOAD (This is where the work is performed.)
##

'''
Abstraction for board squares

 cell ids
+---+---+---+
! 0 | 1 | 2 |
+---+---+---+
! 3 | 4 | 5 |
+---+---+---+
! 6 | 7 | 8 |
+---+---+---+
```

Script 12.2, Abstractions and configurations

154

Then we define how we represent the status of the squares. I decided that the status of individual squares (or the table as a whole) should be stored in an eight element array[10]. We then use the following values to indicate the status of the squares, as represented in the array.

```
###############################
# Board Status Definitions
#   "." = Empty
#   "O" = Us
#   "X" = Opponent
```

Script 12.2, Square status definitions

What results is a one-to-one relationship between array elements and the squares in the game.

Defining how we work with the target's attributes

Since this isn't the first piece of software we've written, we can assume that there are specific things our bot will want to do in the course of a game. These items are found in a library file named `libGame.py`. That file is imported with the code in Script 12.3.

```
sys.path.insert(0, "libs") # Import local libraries
import libGame
```

Script 12.3. Importing the game library

The game library contains those functions that the game will have to perform over and over. Institutionalizing, and limited, these functions is fundamental to writing well documented production-ready code. The four functions that the library provides are described below.

ARRboard = **initBoard()**

This function initializes a new game board array, by setting each array element to a period, indicating that the square is occupied by neither an "X" nor an "O".

showBoard(ARRboard**)**

---

10   Or a "list", in Python. *(Old habits die hard.)*

The showBoard() function writes the status of the current board to the logs. This is essential for debugging as it can be used to log each play of the game.

```
ARRboard = readBoard()
```

The bot reads the status of the board, as it appears in the browser, with the readBoard() function. This function essentially places Os and Xs into the ARRBoard array as they relate to their status and position on the browser.

```
ID = nextMove(ARRboard)
```

Moves are made by the bot with the nextMove() function. This code decides where to make the next move, based on the current board status.

Code walk-through

We've cheated a little bit with this code review because the configuration part has already been covered in the previous paragraphs. This was done to emphasize the importance of looking ahead, examining your target, and determining your approach.

Initializing a match

The game starts as the bot loads the game board from the website. The board is initialized, and the first move is made by selecting a random number between zero and eight, to represent the ID of a square, as shown below.

```
####################################################
# STARTOF Game

libBot.writeLog(logFile, "Loading Game")
url = "http://www.mepso.com/publishing/selenium_python/examples/gameOn/"
driver.get(url)

libBot.randomWait(logFile, 2, 3)

# Initialize board
libBot.writeLog(logFile, "Initialize board")
ARRboard = libGame.initBoard()
libGame.showBoard(logFile, ARRboard)

# Make first move
libBot.writeLog(logFile, "Make the first (random) move")
firstMoveID = randint(0, 8)
libBot.writeLog(logFile, "Our first move is: " + str(firstMoveID) )
```

```
driver.find_element(By.ID, firstMoveID).click()
```
Script 12.4, Making the first move

Immediately after our bot makes its first move, the game responds this it's move.

Subsequent moves

Once the first exchange of moves is made, the bot enters a while loop that continues to play the game until a winner is decided, or on a tie.

This process of playing after the first move is comprised of:

- Reading the current board status,

- Making the next move, and

- Seeing if the game is over, as shown in the following script.

```
gameOver = False
moveCounter=0
while gameOver==False:
    libBot.randomWait(logFile, 2, 3)
    moveCounter = moveCounter +1

    print("moveCounter "+str(moveCounter))
    ARRboard = libGame.readBoard(driver)
    libGame.showBoard(logFile, ARRboard)

    nextMoveID = libGame.nextMove(ARRboard)
    libBot.writeLog(logFile, "The next move is cell: "+str(nextMoveID))
    driver.find_element(By.ID, nextMoveID).click()
    libBot.randomWait(logFile, 2, 3)

    # See if the game is over
    html = libBot.getWebpageContents(logFile, driver)
    libBot.writeFile(logFile, "html.txt", html)

    if libParse.stristr(html, "You lose"):
        libBot.writeLog(logFile, "We lost!")
        gameOver = True

    elif libParse.stristr(html, "You win"):
        libBot.writeLog(logFile, "We win!")
        gameOver = True

    elif libParse.stristr(html, "Tie game"):
    libBot.writeLog(logFile, "We tied!")
```

```
    gameOver = True
```

Script 12.5, The main game loop

The end of the game

The bot decides if the game is over by looking for the existence of specific words on the web page. Selenium doesn't have an issue with reading active content like this, and in our case, we fetch a fresh page with the `libBot.getWebpageContents()` function. The existence of the strings "You lose", You win", and "We tied!" determine when the game is over and the loop is broken.

Once the game is over, the program falls through the while loop and leaves the payload section of the framework.

```
# Show the final board
libBot.writeLog(logFile, "Final Board")
ARRboard = libGame.readBoard(driver)
libGame.showBoard(logFile, ARRboard)
libBot.randomWait(logFile, 9, 10)

# ENDOF Game
########################################################################
```

Script 12.6 Closing the game

The logs

One nice feature of this example is the exquisite logs that are generated. I've stated several times that logs are sometimes your saving grace when you have to debug issues that happened in the past, or irregularly. These logs will take on a new function in the next chapter where we play this game in headless mode.

```
1    2023-05-15 13:29:29: ##############################################
2    2023-05-15 13:29:29: # gameOn.py
3    2023-05-15 13:29:29: ##############################################
4    2023-05-15 13:29:29: Log file: LOG_20230515_132929.log
5    2023-05-15 13:29:29: Loading chromedriver
6    2023-05-15 13:29:35: Setting window size to 800px by 800px.
7    2023-05-15 13:29:35: Positioning window to 10, 10.
8    2023-05-15 13:29:35: Loading Game
9    2023-05-15 13:29:35: Waiting 3
10   2023-05-15 13:29:37: Initialize board
11   2023-05-15 13:29:37: +---+---+---+
12   2023-05-15 13:29:37: | . | . | . |
13   2023-05-15 13:29:37: +---+---+---+
14   2023-05-15 13:29:37: | . | . | . |
15   2023-05-15 13:29:37: +---+---+---+
16   2023-05-15 13:29:37: | . | . | . |
17   2023-05-15 13:29:37: +---+---+---+
18   2023-05-15 13:29:37: Make the first (random) move
19   2023-05-15 13:29:37: Our first move is: 5
20   2023-05-15 13:29:39: Waiting 2
21   2023-05-15 13:29:41: +---+---+---+
22   2023-05-15 13:29:41: | . | . | X |
23   2023-05-15 13:29:41: +---+---+---+
24   2023-05-15 13:29:41: | . | . | O |
25   2023-05-15 13:29:41: +---+---+---+
26   2023-05-15 13:29:41: | . | . | . |
27   2023-05-15 13:29:41: +---+---+---+
28   2023-05-15 13:29:41: The next move is cell: 8
29   2023-05-15 13:29:41: Waiting 3
30   2023-05-15 13:29:43: Capturing screen contents
31   2023-05-15 13:29:43: Writing file: html.txt
32   2023-05-15 13:29:43: Waiting 3
33   2023-05-15 13:29:45: +---+---+---+
34   2023-05-15 13:29:45: | X | . | X |
35   2023-05-15 13:29:45: +---+---+---+
36   2023-05-15 13:29:45: | . | . | O |
37   2023-05-15 13:29:45: +---+---+---+
38   2023-05-15 13:29:45: | . | . | O |
39   2023-05-15 13:29:45: +---+---+---+
40   2023-05-15 13:29:45: The next move is cell: 1
41   2023-05-15 13:29:45: Waiting 2
42   2023-05-15 13:29:46: Capturing screen contents
43   2023-05-15 13:29:46: Writing file: html.txt
44   2023-05-15 13:29:46: Waiting 2
45   2023-05-15 13:29:48: +---+---+---+
46   2023-05-15 13:29:48: | X | O | X |
47   2023-05-15 13:29:48: +---+---+---+
48   2023-05-15 13:29:48: | . | . | O |
49   2023-05-15 13:29:48: +---+---+---+
50   2023-05-15 13:29:48: | X | . | O |
51   2023-05-15 13:29:48: +---+---+---+
52   2023-05-15 13:29:48: The next move is cell: 4
53   2023-05-15 13:29:48: Waiting 3
54   2023-05-15 13:29:50: Capturing screen contents
55   2023-05-15 13:29:50: Writing file: html.txt
56   2023-05-15 13:29:50: We lost!
57   2023-05-15 13:29:50: Final Board
58   2023-05-15 13:29:50: +---+---+---+
59   2023-05-15 13:29:50: | X | O | X |
60   2023-05-15 13:29:50: +---+---+---+
61   2023-05-15 13:29:50: | X | O | O |
62   2023-05-15 13:29:50: +---+---+---+
63   2023-05-15 13:29:50: | X | . | O |
64   2023-05-15 13:29:50: +---+---+---+
65   2023-05-15 13:29:50: Waiting 9
66   2023-05-15 13:29:58: Shutting down program: gameOn.py
67   2023-05-15 13:29:58: Execution time: 29.01 seconds.
```

Figure 12.3, The logs generated by this bot

Question...

We've seen earlier how Selenium can interact with the JavaScript that is on a target webpage. This topic is covered in some detail in Chapter 15, " *DOM and JavaScript*".

Since Selenium can directly execute JavaScript that is on a target webpage, would it be possible to cheat on the game by using Selenium to directly call the JavaScript functions or manipulate JavaScript variables? I haven't looked at the target JavaScript well enough to know if this is possible. If you find that it is, please leave a note at this project's video.

Script: gameOn.py

```
######################################################################
scriptName = "gameOn" + ".py"
#---------------------------

# # # # # # # # # # # # # #
# Configuration
import   sys
import   os
import   time

from     datetime import datetime
from     random   import randint

import   selenium
from     selenium.webdriver.common.by import By
from     selenium.webdriver.common.keys import Keys

# # # # # # # # # # # # # # #
# Record the start time
start_time = time.time()
timeStart = datetime.today().strftime('%Y%m%d_%H%M%S')

# # # # # # # # # # # # # # #
# Establish paths and import libraries
#
sys.path.insert(0, "../../libs")              # Import local libraries
from libPaths            import logFile
from libPaths            import pathChromeDriver

import libBot            # Useful bot functions

import libParse          # Parse functions

import libSelenium          # Selenium (chromedriver) specific functions


# # # # # # # # # # # # # # #
# Manage Logs
try:
        os.system("rm *.log")
except:
        libBot.writeLog(logFile, "There were no log files to remove.")

print("\n")
libBot.writeLog(logFile, "###########################################")
libBot.writeLog(logFile, "# " + scriptName)
libBot.writeLog(logFile, "###########################################")
libBot.writeLog(logFile, "Log file: " + logFile)

# Load Selenium (get driver) and resize/reposition the browser window
driver = libSelenium.loadWebdriver(logFile, pathChromeDriver)
```

161

```
libSelenium.setWindowSize(logFile, driver, x=800, y=800)
libSelenium.setWindowPosition(logFile, driver, x=10, y=10)

###########################################################################
###########################################################################
## Start: PAYLOAD (This is where the work is performed.)
##

'''
        cell ids
              +---+---+---+
              ! 0 | 1 | 2 |
              +---+---+---+
              ! 3 | 4 | 5 |
              +---+---+---+
              ! 6 | 7 | 8 |
              +---+---+---+
'''

sys.path.insert(0, "libs")                    # Import local libraries
import libGame


###################################################
# STARTOF Game

libBot.writeLog(logFile, "Loading Game")
url = "http://www.mepso.com/publishing/selenium_python/examples/gameOn/"
driver.get(url)

libBot.randomWait(logFile, 2, 3)

# Initialize board
slibBot.writeLog(logFile, "Initialize board")
ARRboard = libGame.initBoard(logFile)
libGame.showBoard(logFile, ARRboard)

# Make first move
libBot.writeLog(logFile, "Make the first (random) move")
firstMoveID = randint(0, 8)
libBot.writeLog(logFile, "Our first move is: " + str(firstMoveID) )
driver.find_element(By.ID, firstMoveID).click()


gameOver = False
move=0
while gameOver==False:

        libBot.randomWait(logFile, 2, 3)

        move = move +1

        print("Move "+str(move))
```

162

```
        ARRboard = libGame.readBoard(logFile, driver)
        libGame.showBoard(logFile, ARRboard)

        nextMoveID = libGame.nextMove(ARRboard)
        libBot.writeLog(logFile, "The next move is cell: "+str(nextMoveID))
        driver.find_element(By.ID, nextMoveID).click()
        libBot.randomWait(logFile, 2, 3)

        # See if the game is over
        html = libBot.getWebpageContents(logFile, driver)
        libBot.writeFile(logFile, "html.txt", html)

        if libParse.stristr(html, "You lose"):
                libBot.writeLog(logFile, "We lost!")
                gameOver = True

        elif libParse.stristr(html, "You win"):
                libBot.writeLog(logFile, "We win!")
                gameOver = True

        elif libParse.stristr(html, "Tie game"):
                libBot.writeLog(logFile, "We tied!")
                gameOver = True

# Show the final board
libBot.writeLog(logFile, "Final Board")
ARRboard = libGame.readBoard(logFile, driver)
libGame.showBoard(logFile, ARRboard)
libBot.randomWait(logFile, 9, 10)

# ENDOF Payload
########################################################################
########################################################################

# # # # # # # # # # # # # #
# Close gracefully
libBot.closeBot(logFile, driver, "Exiting normally: "+scriptName)
########################################################################
```

Script 12.6, The gameOn.py script

Script: libGame.py

```
#####################################################################
# libGame
#-------------------------------------------------------------------
# Library for gameOn.py
#(must be in same directory as gameOn.py)
#####################################################################

import   sys
import   selenium
from      selenium.webdriver.common.by import By

sys.path.insert(0, "../../libs")            # Import local libraries
import   libBot

################################
# initBoard( logFile )
################################
def initBoard(logFile):
        libBot.writeLog(logFile, "Initializing board")

        brd = [0] * 9              # initialize a nine element array
        indexes = range(9)
        for cellId in indexes:
                brd[cellId] = "."

        return brd

# endof: initBoard()
#----------------------------


################################
# readBoard( logFile, driver )
################################
def readBoard(logFile, driver):
        libBot.writeLog(logFile, "Reading board")

        brd = [0] * 9              # initialize a nine element array
        indexes = range(9)
        for cellId in indexes:
                brd[cellId] = driver.find_element(By.ID, cellId).get_attribute('innerHTML')
                if(brd[cellId]) == "":
                        brd[cellId] = "."

        return brd

# endof: readBoard()
#----------------------------


################################
# showBoard( logFile, board_array)
```

164

```
###############################
def showBoard(logFile, brd):
        libBot.writeLog(logFile, "+---+---+---+")
        libBot.writeLog(logFile, "| " + brd[0] +" | "+ brd[1] +" | " + brd[2] + " | " )
        libBot.writeLog(logFile, "+---+---+---+")
        libBot.writeLog(logFile, "| " + brd[3] +" | "+ brd[4] +" | " + brd[5] + " | " )
        libBot.writeLog(logFile, "+---+---+---+")
        libBot.writeLog(logFile, "| " + brd[6] +" | "+ brd[7] +" | " + brd[8] + " | " )
        libBot.writeLog(logFile, "+---+---+---+")

# endof: showBoard()
#----------------------------


###############################
# nextMove( board_array)
###############################
def nextMove(brd):

        '''
                    cell ids
                      +---+---+---+
                      ! 0 | 1 | 2 |
                      +---+---+---+
                      ! 3 | 4 | 5 |
                      +---+---+---+
                      ! 6 | 7 | 8 |
                      +---+---+---+
        '''

        nextMoveId = 99
        us = "O"
        them = "X"
        empty = "."

        # Virtical
        if brd[1]==them and brd[2]==them and brd[0]==empty:
                nextMoveId = 0
        if brd[0]==them and brd[2]==them and brd[1]==empty:
                nextMoveId = 1
        if brd[0]==them and brd[1]==them and brd[2]==empty:
                nextMoveId = 2

        if brd[4]==them and brd[5]==them and brd[3]==empty:
                nextMoveId = 3
        if brd[3]==them and brd[5]==them and brd[4]==empty:
                nextMoveId = 4
        if brd[3]==them and brd[4]==them and brd[5]==empty:
                nextMoveId = 5

        if brd[7]==them and brd[8]==them and brd[6]==empty:
                nextMoveId = 6
        if brd[6]==them and brd[8]==them and brd[7]==empty:
                nextMoveId = 7
```

165

```
            if brd[6]==them and brd[7]==them and brd[8]==empty:
                    nextMoveId = 8

        # Horizontal
        if brd[3]==them and brd[6]==them and brd[0]==empty:
                nextMoveId = 0
        if brd[0]==them and brd[6]==them and brd[3]==empty:
                nextMoveId = 3
        if brd[0]==them and brd[3]==them and brd[6]==empty:
                nextMoveId = 6

        if brd[4]==them and brd[7]==them and brd[1]==empty:
                nextMoveId = 1
        if brd[1]==them and brd[7]==them and brd[4]==empty:
                nextMoveId = 4
        if brd[1]==them and brd[4]==them and brd[7]==empty:
                nextMoveId = 7

        if brd[5]==them and brd[8]==them and brd[2]==empty:
                nextMoveId = 2
        if brd[2]==them and brd[8]==them and brd[5]==empty:
                nextMoveId = 5
        if brd[2]==them and brd[5]==them and brd[8]==empty:
                nextMoveId = 8

        # Diagonal
        if brd[4]==them and brd[8]==them and brd[0]==empty:
                nextMoveId = 0
        if brd[0]==them and brd[4]==them and brd[8]==empty:
                nextMoveId = 8
        if brd[0]==them and brd[8]==them and brd[4]==empty:
                nextMoveId = 4

        if brd[4]==them and brd[6]==them and brd[2]==empty:
                nextMoveId = 2
        if brd[2]==them and brd[6]==them and brd[4]==empty:
                nextMoveId = 4
        if brd[2]==them and brd[4]==them and brd[6]==empty:
                nextMoveId = 6

        if nextMoveId==99:
                indexes = range(9)
                for cellId in indexes:
                        if brd[cellId]!=them and brd[cellId]!=us:
                                    nextMoveId = cellId

        return nextMoveId

# endof: nextMove()
#----------------------------
```

Script 12.7, The libGame.py script.

## CHAPTER 13

PROJ 10: HEADLESS BROWSING

The thing that makes Selenium amazing is that it allows developers to directly control the actions of browsers. But sometimes, using a browser is a liability. In fact, there are many reasons why it can be advantageous to run bots in a headless, (non browser) mode.

This chapter explores what Selenium Headless Mode is, and it's benefits and limitations. We will also be using the game that was explored in the previous chapter. That example will be prefect for this headless implementation because of it's use of graphics, which we won't see in headless mode, and the explicit logging, which we will see in headless mode.

Watch the associated video on YouTube

There is an associated video on YouTube where you can watch demonstration of this bot as well as see a narrated code walk-through. Go to www.mepso.com and click on the link for this book on the home page. You'll find links to videos and library downloads there.

Figure 13.1, Link to chapter video

The link above will redirect you to an "unlisted" video with both a project demonstration and a code walk-through are available for your use. If you find something interesting in your development, please feel free to leave a message in the video's comment section.

What is headless mode?

Headless mode is a way to run Selenium without actually seeing the browser window. It allows automated tests or web scraping tasks to be performed at a command prompt, without any visible user interface.

Think of it like a computer program that can interact with websites and perform tasks just like a person would, but without needing to open a browser window.

Selenium, in headless mode, operates within a shell or command window, accessing web pages, clicking buttons, filling out forms, and extracting information, all without any visual evidence of a browser.

Headless mode is useful because it can execute tasks faster and use fewer system resources compared to running a browser with a visible interface. It's like having an invisible browser that can perform tasks more efficiently. This makes it great for running tests or performing automated tasks on servers, where a graphical interface is not necessary or may not even be available.

If there's no browser, what is there?

When you run a Selenium program in headless mode, no browser appears during program execution, but everything else remains the same. All of the same Selenium controls are in effect, you can even emulate specific browsers through your selection of Webdriver. The only difference is you don't see a browser, because there is no browser in headless mode.

Advantages of headless mode

Running Selenium in headless mode, which means running the browser without a graphical user interface (GUI), offers several advantages as spelled out below.

- Headless mode eliminates the overhead of rendering and displaying the browser GUI, resulting in faster test execution. Without the need to render graphics, the browser operations are generally more efficient, leading to improved performance.

- Headless mode consumes fewer system resources (CPU, memory) compared to running the browser with a GUI. This allows for easier resource management, especially when running multiple tests concurrently or on machines with limited resources.

- Headless mode facilitates running tests on a large scale. Since headless browsers require fewer system resources, it becomes easier to execute tests in parallel across multiple virtual machines or containers, leading to improved scalability and reduced test execution time.

- Headless mode is particularly useful for server-side automation, where running a browser with a GUI is unnecessary or impractical. It allows for seamless integration with Continuous Integration/Continuous Deployment (CI/CD) pipelines, where automated tests can be executed on servers or in headless environments without user interaction.

- Headless mode enables testing and web scraping on platforms that may not have a GUI, such as Linux-based systems. This expands the range of testing scenarios and allows for comprehensive compatibility testing across different environments.

- Probably the biggest reason to run Selenium in headless mode is because it can substantially reduce hosting costs. By leveraging headless mode, organizations can save costs on infrastructure, as there is no need for physical machines or virtual machines with graphical capabilities. Headless browsers can be run on lightweight servers or in cloud-based environments, reducing infrastructure costs.

Overall, running Selenium in headless mode offers faster execution, improved resource utilization, enhanced scalability, and compatibility across various platforms. It is particularly beneficial for server-side automation, large-scale test execution, and scenarios where a GUI is not required or feasible.

Disadvantages of headless mode

The previous paragraphs outlined a lot of reasons for running Selenium in headless mode. And, you may be wondering, "What's the downside?"

The following outlines a few reasons why not every project should be run in Selenium headless mode.

- Troubleshooting and debugging issues can be more difficult in headless mode since there is no visible browser window to observe actions or diagnose problems visually. Identifying the root cause of failures or unexpected behavior may require additional logging and analysis.

- In headless mode, you cannot visually verify the appearance and layout of web pages. If your tests or tasks involve verifying visual elements, such as checking the placement of elements, colors, or fonts, it may be challenging to perform visual validation in a headless environment.

- Headless browsers may have limited or different support for JavaScript compared to their graphical counterparts. Some JavaScript-intensive websites or applications may behave differently or encounter compatibility issues in headless mode. This can affect the accuracy and reliability of your tests.

- Working with headless mode may require additional technical expertise or familiarity with command-line interfaces, as you often interact with Selenium and configure headless browsers using code or terminal commands.

- While headless browsers strive to be compatible with standard browsers, there may still be subtle differences in behavior or rendering between headless mode and real browsers. These differences could potentially impact the accuracy and reliability of your tests or web scraping tasks.

Knowledge of Selenium headless mode, and how to implement it, is an important tool to have in your botDev toolkit. But it's also important to evaluate these disadvantages in the context of your specific use case and determine if the trade-offs are acceptable. Depending on your testing requirements or specific application, running Selenium in a graphical mode may be more suitable, allowing for visual validation and better simulation of user interactions.

How headless mode it typically used

Typically the driving reason to use Selenium in headless mode is to reduce hosting costs. Because, if one can run a bot on a simple AWS tiny Linux instance, it's probably preferable to a more expensive windowed environment, especially if the project needs to scale to fifty, or more, bots.

Here are some suggestions for using headless mode in your own practice.

Develop in regular browser mode

In most of these circumstances, bots are developed in the standard (non-headless) mode where the bowser is fully available. This not only makes it easier to evaluate bot performance, but it also avails the developer to browser-based tools like the Selenium IDE plug-in and Chrome Inspect.

Validate and deploy in headless mode

Once the bot is running as designed (and the design is proven to satisfy the design requirements), it is only a single line of code that converts a Selenium program to headless mode.

The need for accurate and informative logging—as defined by the framework, early in Section II, is of paramount importance when running Selenium in headless mode. This is one of the reasons the game playing bot was chosen for this example. That bot is very visual, yet it can be very easily monitored by using the log file created by the framework.

Our headless Selenium example

That little framework we established in Section II allows for easy conversion to headless mode, as how in the following code snippet.

```
# Load Selenium (get driver)

# HEADLESS
driver = libSelenium.loadHeadlessWebdriver(logFile, pathChromeDriver)

# STANDARD
driver = libSelenium.loadWebdriver(logFile, pathChromeDriver)
```
Script 13.1, Converting a Selenium Python program to headless mode

The line of code, above, that creates the headless version of the program uses a wrapper function called `loadHeadslessWebdriver()` from the `libSelenium` library.

The line of code, shown in Script 13.1, shows how headless mode is actually implemented. This function inserts headless mode as an option that is loaded while configuring the Webdriver instance.

```
def loadHeadlessWebdriver(logFile, pathChromeDriver):
        options = Webdriver.ChromeOptions()
        options.add_argument("--headless=new")

        libBot.writeLog(logFile, "Loading headless chromedriver")
        service = Webdriver.chrome.service.Service(executable_path=pathChromeDriver)
        service.start()
        driver = Webdriver.Chrome(service=service, options=options)

        return driver
```

Script 13.2, The function that implements headless mode

Once the Webdriver is loaded in headless mode, the bot will run without the need for a browser.

The Code walk-through

It feels a little anticlimactic to end this section of projects this way, but the code change to headless mode, in Script 13.2, is essentially the code walk-through.

Project conclusion

If you haven't already done so, I encourage you to develop both this project, as well as the previous one. Because, once you see the script run in both regular, and headless modes, it's kind'a magical to watch.

I also encourage you to watch the video for this project, as found on www.mepso.com.

Script: headless.py

```
#####################################################################
scriptName = "headless" + ".py"
#---------------------------

# # # # # # # # # # # # # # #
# Configuration
import  sys
import  os
import  time

from    datetime import datetime
from    random   import randint

import  selenium
from    selenium.webdriver.common.by import By
from    selenium.webdriver.common.keys import Keys

# # # # # # # # # # # # # # #
# Record the start time
start_time = time.time()
timeStart = datetime.today().strftime('%Y%m%d_%H%M%S')

# # # # # # # # # # # # # # #
# Establish paths and import libraries
#
sys.path.insert(0, "../../libs")        # Import local libraries
from libPaths              import logFile
from libPaths              import pathChromeDriver
from libPaths         import pathRoot

import libBot              # Useful bot functions
import libParse            # Parse functions
import libSelenium         # Selenium (chromedriver) specific functions

# # # # # # # # # # # # # # #
# Manage Logs
try:
        os.system("delete *.log")
except:
        libBot.writeLog(logFile, "There were no log files to remove.")

print("\n")
libBot.writeLog(logFile, "###########################################")
libBot.writeLog(logFile, "# " + scriptName)
libBot.writeLog(logFile, "###########################################")
libBot.writeLog(logFile, "Log file: " + logFile)

# Load Selenium (get driver) and resize/reposition the browser window
driver = libSelenium.loadWebdriver(logFile, pathChromeDriver)
libSelenium.setWindowSize(logFile, driver, x=800, y=800)
libSelenium.setWindowPosition(logFile, driver, x=10, y=10)
```

```
#########################################################################
#########################################################################
## Start: PAYLOAD (This is where the work is performed.)
##

'''
          cell ids
                +---+---+---+
                ! 0 | 1 | 2 |
                +---+---+---+
                ! 3 | 4 | 5 |
                +---+---+---+
                ! 6 | 7 | 8 |
                +---+---+---+
'''

sys.path.insert(0, pathRoot)              # Import local libraries
import libGame


####################################################
# START OF Game

libBot.writeLog(logFile, "Loading Game")
url = "http://www.mepso.com/publishing/selenium_python/examples/gameOn/"
driver.get(url)

libBot.randomWait(logFile, 2, 3)

# Initialize board
libBot.writeLog(logFile, "Initialize board")
ARRboard = libGame.initBoard()
libGame.showBoard(logFile, driver, ARRboard, move="0")

# Make first move
libBot.writeLog(logFile, "Make the first (random) move")
firstMoveID = randint(0,8)
firstMoveID = 4;
libBot.writeLog(logFile, "Our first move is: " + str(firstMoveID) )
driver.find_element(By.ID, firstMoveID).click()


gameOver = False
move=0
while gameOver==False:

        libBot.randomWait(logFile, 2, 3)

        move = move +1

        libBot.writeLog(logFile, "Move "+str(move))
        ARRboard = libGame.readBoard(driver)
```

```
        libGame.showBoard(logFile, driver, ARRboard, str(move))

        nextMoveID = libGame.nextMove(ARRboard)
        libBot.writeLog(logFile, "The next move is cell: "+str(nextMoveID))
        driver.find_element(By.ID, nextMoveID).click()
        libBot.randomWait(logFile, 2, 3)

        # See if the game is over
        html = libBot.getWebpageContents(logFile, driver)
        libBot.writeFile(logFile, "html.txt", html)

        if libParse.stristr(html, "You lose"):
                libBot.writeLog(logFile, "We lost!")
                gameOver = True

        elif libParse.stristr(html, "You win"):
                libBot.writeLog(logFile, "We win!")
                gameOver = True

        elif libParse.stristr(html, "Tie game"):
                libBot.writeLog(logFile, "We tied!")
                gameOver = True


# Show the final board
libBot.writeLog(logFile, "Final Board")
ARRboard = libGame.readBoard(driver)
libGame.showBoard(logFile, driver, ARRboard, str(move))
libBot.randomWait(logFile, 9, 10)


# ENDOF Payload
##########################################################################
##########################################################################

# # # # # # # # # # # # # # #
# Close gracefully
libBot.closeBot(logFile, driver, "Exiting normally: "+scriptName)
##########################################################################
```

Script 13.3, The full script: headless.py

Section III: Theory

While the previous section focused on getting you up and running as soon as possible, this section is intended to be more deliberate and thought provoking. Here, you will find ten additional areas of botOps that you should be aware of before you pursue a career as a bot developer.

CHAPTER *14*, *STAYING OUT OF JAIL*

Bot development offers exciting opportunities to not only access vast amounts of data but also control and automate online services. It is essential, however, to recognize that, in many cases, data and services belong to other individuals and organizations. And there are laws that protect the original owners rights to use those services and that data exclusively.

You may be fired-up to do some crazy things, armed with the information and new skills you acquired from this book. But it's important to apply the brakes here and stress that violating peoples intellectual property rights is a path to either, paying high fines, or a stay in jail.

Before diving deep into bot development, it is crucial to understand what data and services you can legally collect and use, as well as what data is off-limits.

I must emphasize that this chapter does not constitute legal advice. However, over the years I have sought guidance from attorneys and have had a few experiences in my private practice. Consider this information as a collection of suggestions rather than anything that resembles formal legal counsel.

I don't want to either overplay, nor underplay, the legal exposure one assumes when they either commission, or develop, a bot. Personally, I've never ran into any real legal issues as a bot developer. But much of that is because I've been careful, and take the advise of experts outside of my field.

ProTip!
One essential piece of advice I can offer is that attorneys are litigious by nature. If they suspect that you have infringed upon their clients' rights, they won't hesitate to pursue legal action. Thus, it is wise to familiarize yourself with relevant laws to know what questions to ask

when seeking legal assistance. The other advice I have is to get an attorney before you need one!

As you scrape information from the Internet, it's good to know that not everything is there for your taking. Various types of *intellectual property rights*, either Patent, Copyright, Trademark, or Trade Secrets may prevent you from using data, even though you were able to collect it.

Much of intellectual property law, or IP, is less an issue of who filed papers to protect their idea, and more of what the end user (potential infringer) plans to do with it. In other words, intent often clouds intellectual property law.

Here is a break down of the basic vehicles people use to protect ideas and data,.

Patents

An individual or organization has the option to disclose an idea to the public through a lengthy and costly process known as patenting. This process ensures that the owner will have a legally protected monopoly on the use of that idea for a specific period. Patents fall under the category of Intellectual Property, but they are the least relevant aspect when it comes to bots.

Copyright

A copyright is a type of legal protection granted to authors or creators of original works, encompassing literary, artistic, musical, and other intellectual creations. Copyright protection is automatic and comes into effect as soon as an original work is created and expressed in a tangible form, such as writing, painting, recording, or digital storage. Proof of the date of creation rests on the creator, but it isn't that hard to establish when something was written or drawn.

Under copyright law, the creator of an original work is granted exclusive rights to reproduce, distribute, publicly display, publicly perform, and create derivative works based on the original work. These rights allow the creator to control how their work is used, shared, and monetized, and to protect their work from unauthorized copying or use.

Copyright protection lasts for a limited period, usually the life of the author plus a certain number of years after their death (typically 70 years in the United States and many other countries)[11]. After the copyright term expires, the work enters the public domain, and anyone can freely use, share, or build upon the work without needing permission from the original creator.

You can't copyright a fact

It is important to note that copyright law protects the expression of ideas, not the ideas themselves[12]. Facts, concepts, and ideas are not subject to copyright protection, but the way they are presented in an original work (such as the unique arrangement of words in a book or the composition of a photograph) can be protected by copyright. For example, one could copyright a directory of people and their email addresses. But you cannot copyright the names and email addresses themselves because both the names and email address are facts. What is protectable is the style and format of those directories.

In many countries, including the United States, registering a copyright with a government agency is not required to obtain copyright protection. However, registration can provide additional benefits, such as facilitating the ability to sue for copyright infringement and seek statutory damages.

The most important message from the previous passage is that you cannot copyright a fact. Since much of what you're apt to be collecting are facts, you shouldn't be prevented by any law from using those facts.

Facts commonly collected by bots

Bots often collect PII, or Personally Identifiable Information. This includes items like names, email addresses, license IDs, and phone numbers. People may want to keep identifiers like Government Identification Numbers secret. And it's a

---

11   *How long does a copyright last*. Copyright Alliance. (2023, June 15). https://copyrightalliance.org/faqs/how-long-does-copyright-last

12   *What does copyright protect?*. What Does Copyright Protect? (FAQ) | U.S. Copyright Office. (n.d.). https://www.copyright.gov/help/faq/faq-protect.html#:~:text=Copyright%20does%20not%20protect%20facts,way%20these%20things%20are%20expressed.

good idea to do so because there is no law to protect these assets once they are disclosed.

Prices and inventory levels of online stores are a common target for bots, in efforts to collect market and even sales data. This data can help retailers manage prices and selection. Careful collections like these can reveal your competitors sales strategies, supply line issues, and distribution schemes.

Many times bots look for the dates and times that specific events happen. And while there may be aspects of an event that involve intellectual property rights (like the Olympics) the date at which an event occurs is in the public domain.

Job postings, that appear on web pages are also a common bot target. If it's important for you to know that your competitor is hiring for a new technology in a new town, you can probably get that information—legally—from their job postings.

Facts are considered objective pieces of information that exist independently of any individual's creative expression. Since facts are discovered rather than created, they are considered part of the public domain, and anyone is free to use, share, or build upon them. Granting copyright protection to facts would hinder the free flow of information, restrict access to knowledge, and impede scientific and cultural progress.

However the format in which facts are presented, such as in a book or article, can be protected by copyright if the presentation meets the threshold of originality. In this case, the author holds the copyright on the creative expression and arrangement of the facts, not the facts themselves. Other individuals are free to use the same facts in their work, as long as they don't copy the original author's unique expression or presentation.

Other exceptions to copyright

In addition to the exclusion of facts, US copyright law has other fairly broad exceptions that allow the use of copyrighted material without the need for explicit permission from the copyright holder. Some of the key exceptions include:

Fair Use

This is perhaps the most well-known exception of copyright. Fair use allows for the use of copyrighted material for purposes such as criticism, commentary, news reporting, teaching, scholarship, and research. The determination of fair use involves considering factors like the purpose of the use, the nature of the copyrighted work, the amount used, and the effect on the market for the original work.

Public Domain

Works in the public domain are not protected by copyright and are free for anyone to use. This encompasses works with expired copyrights, those that were never eligible for copyright protection, and works for which the copyright holder has explicitly relinquished their rights. The duration of copyright protection varies depending on the medium, so you may be able to use intellectual property that received copyright protection many years ago, but it's always advisable to verify the status beforehand.

People, who watch for when specific pieces of literature enter the Public Domain. They have started to call New Years Day, Public Domain Day[13]. Every year, several classic books and movies enter the realm of unprotected.

Creative Commons Licenses

Some copyright holders choose to license their works under Creative Commons licenses, which allow certain uses of their work while retaining some rights. These licenses come with various levels of permissions, such as allowing non-commercial use, requiring attribution, or permitting derivative works. For example, the scripts at the end of this book, are protected by the W3C License, which specifically states that the user of the product is completely responsible for its use.

---

13 *How long does a copyright last*. Copyright Alliance. (2023, June 15).
     https://copyrightalliance.org/faqs/how-long-does-copyright-last

Educational Use

There are specific exceptions for using copyrighted material in an educational setting, like in classroom teaching, online courses, or distance education. These exceptions are not universal and subject to certain limitations.

Library and Archives

Copyright law allows libraries and archives to make copies of copyrighted materials for purposes such as preservation, research, and providing access to patrons.

This is also a good example that proves that not all of these exemptions are absolute. For example, a federal judge recently ruled in favor of the four prominent U.S. publishers[14], who filed a lawsuit against the Internet Archive for its actions during the early days of the COVID-19 pandemic. The nonprofit, also known as *The Wayback Machine*, had scanned and provided free access to numerous digital copies of copyrighted books through the creation of the National Emergency Library, which was operational from March 24, 2020, to June 16, 2020.

The Internet Archive justified the launch of the National Emergency Library as a means to assist individuals who had lost access to physical libraries due to the pandemic. However, this initiative involved the simultaneous lending of multiple digital copies of the same book. In response, the four publishers filed a lawsuit covering one hundred twenty-four books from this collection, asserting that the Internet Archive's actions constituted *"mass copyright infringement."* The Internet Archive argued that its actions were legally protected under the fair use doctrine.

Parody and Satire

Copyright law often allows for the use of copyrighted material in parody and satire, as these uses are considered transformative and provide social commentary. It is because of this exclusion that people like Weird Al Yankovic have had successful and long careers.

---

14 https://time.com/6266147/internet-archive-copyright-infringement-books-lawsuit/

News Reporting

Using copyrighted material in news reporting and journalism is generally allowed, as long as it is used to inform the public about current events. This would include the use of short quotes in book reviews, or show movie clips in theater commentary.

Time shifting

Time shifting refers to making personal copies of copyrighted material for later viewing or listening. For example, recording a TV show to watch later or ripping a CD to listen to on a portable device. The implication, however, is that the person doing the time shifting has legal use of the media and that time shifting is the only use of the copied media.

Trespass to Chattels

Unlike the Intellectual Property law we've explored to this point, Trespass to Chattels refers to the use of physical property. Trespass to chattels occurs when someone intentionally interferes with, or damages someone else's property. Trespass to digital chattels is illegal and can result in civil and criminal penalties, including fines, imprisonment, and damages for any harm caused to the victim.

Applies to physical or digital assets

Typically these cases involve the denial of use of physical assets, like a developer cutting off access to a road, or someone illegally parking in the space used by a company vehicle. But these cases extend to digital assets too.

One of the more interesting Trespass to Chattels cases was the case of an unnamed Asian Airline[15] that found a creative way to monopolize markets and raise prices.

Back in 2017, bot developers for an Asian airline came under scrutiny for a practice where partial reservations were made on rival airlines' websites. This was done with the intention of preventing the sale of those particular tickets. They had discovered that

---

15 Believe me, I have tried to identify the airline, but for now this story will be shrouded in online controversy. I suspect the airline would do better without the publicity. From the best I can cypher, the airline was somewhere in Southeast Asia.

when a person added a ticket to their online shopping cart on the reservation system, the airline held the ticket for a span of fifteen minutes. During this time, the ticket was set aside for potential purchase and was not accessible to other customers. If the fifteen minutes elapsed without the ticket being bought, that ticket would become available once more. However, these particular incomplete reservations were created for the express intent to obstruct other airlines from selling these seats. As a result, this action curtailed competition and had the potential to cause an escalation in ticket prices.

The practice was discovered when several airlines noticed a sudden increase in the number of incomplete bookings on their websites, which were later traced back to the airline in question. (This also points out the importance of keeping and analyzing server access logs!)

The incident sparked a broader debate over the use of screen scraping in the travel industry, with some arguing that it is a legitimate business practice that helps companies to access valuable data and improve their services. While others contend that it is a form of intellectual property theft that can harm consumers and limit competition.

Trademarks

Trademarks play a crucial role in our daily lives, even if we might not always be aware of their significance. From the iconic logos of our favorite brands to the names of popular products, trademarks are all around us.

At their core, trademarks are a distinctive sign or symbol that identifies and distinguishes goods or services offered by one seller or provider from those of others. It acts as a symbol of trust, quality, and source, allowing consumers to make informed choices in the marketplace.

Trademarks are essential for businesses and individuals seeking to protect their brand identity and reputation. By securing a trademark, a company can prevent others from using similar marks that might cause confusion among consumers or dilute the brand's distinctiveness. Trademarks can be comprised of words, images, sounds, or even colors.

Trademark owners have the right to enforce their trademarks against unauthorized use or infringement. Infringement occurs when someone else uses a confusingly similar mark for similar goods or services, potentially causing consumer confusion.

Trade secrets

Trade secrets are confidential, proprietary information that gives a business a competitive advantage over its competitors. Trade secrets can encompass a wide range of valuable data, including manufacturing processes, customer lists, marketing strategies, formulas, recipes, and technical know-how. Unlike patents or trademarks, trade secrets remain hidden from public view and provide lasting value as long as they remain undisclosed.

Unlike other forms of intellectual property, trade secrets are protected primarily through confidentiality and security measures. Companies must take active steps to keep their trade secrets secret. This includes implementing robust internal policies, non-disclosure agreements with employees and business partners, and restricted access to sensitive information.

While trade secrets offer distinct advantages, they differ from patents and copyrights in critical ways. Patents grant exclusive rights to inventors for a limited time in exchange for public disclosure of the invention. Copyrights protect original works of authorship but do not cover ideas or procedures. Trade secrets, on the other hand, are not disclosed to the public and have no expiration date, as long as the secrecy is maintained.

There are two general areas where trade secret laws are applied.

> Trade secret theft, also known as misappropriation, occurs when someone gains unauthorized access to confidential information. This would include situations were physical files are stolen or networks are hacked.

> Another crime is when a confidant intentionally discloses secrets to an unauthorized person. When a trade secret is misappropriated, the injured party can seek legal remedies, including injunctive relief to prevent further disclosure and monetary damages to compensate for losses.

Crimes prosecuted under trade secret law can even venture into the area of espionage, if foreign parties are involved.

Reverse engineered trade secrets

Reverse engineering, involves independently analyzing a product or process to understand its underlying technology or methodology. This is done without access to the original design documents or proprietary information. In the context of trade secrets, reverse engineering can be both a legitimate practice and a potential risk.

Reverse engineering is generally legal and is a recognized method of learning about a product or process for purposes such as interoperability or compatibility. Trade secret law does not prohibit competitors from reverse engineering a product to develop their own non-infringing version. If, however, reverse engineering involves improper means, such as unauthorized access to proprietary information[16], it can lead to trade secret misappropriation claims and potential legal consequences.

Independent discovery of trade secrets

Trade secrets are protected under trade secret law as long as they remain secret and the owner takes reasonable steps to keep them confidential. However, trade secret protection does not prevent others from independently developing or discovering the same information through lawful means.

If you independently and legitimately discover a trade secret without any prior knowledge of it, you are not bound by any obligation of confidentiality or restrictions. You are free to use and exploit that information for your own purposes, even if it is the same as someone else's trade secret.

For example, Sam discovered that his main competitor's order numbers were sequential. In other words, if order 20212 was filed, the next order would be 20213. Sam discovered that he could use this information to estimate how many orders his competitor receives in a given month—a potential trade secret. Now, Sam's competitor's trade secret becomes Sam's trade secret...!

---

16   AKA, hacking.

Trade secrets and metadata

As you may have guessed, discovered trade secrets are one of the major goals of botOps and many Competitive Intelligence campaigns. Notice in the last example, that the competing organization's sales figures weren't published, but calculated from discovered data. This type of data is called *Metadata*. Metadata is essentially information that puts other data into context. It is almost always inferred and more closely constitutes evidence (or intelligence) than an actual fact.

The BOTS Act of 2016

As the industry matures, the collection of case law (or legal precedence) grows. But there come times when specific legislation is deemed necessary. The BOTS Act, or the "Better Online Ticket Sales Act of 2016", is a U.S. federal law. Its purpose is to combat the use of automated software or bots to unfairly gain access to tickets for various events such as concerts, sporting events, and theater performances.

These bots are often used by so called *scalpers,* or ticket resellers, to quickly purchase large quantities of tickets as soon as they become available. This practice can lead to rapid sell-outs and inflated prices on secondary markets. The BOTS Act doesn't make ticket resale illegal. Or for that matter, it doesn't make automated ticket purchases illegal either. But it does make it illegal to use such software to circumvent control measures that are in place to ensure "fair access" to tickets. It also prohibits the sale of tickets that have been obtained in violation of the act.

While there wasn't a single case that triggered this law, it is thought that a 2013 concert tour by singer-songwriter Adele brought attention to this issue. Many Adele fans were unable to purchase tickets at face value because bots had bought up large quantities of them, forcing fans to pay exorbitant prices on resale websites. I suspect that this law changed the way bots purchase tickets, but I doubt they stopped buying tickets automatically as it could be very difficult to either prove that the tickets were purchased automatically or that the ticket seller suffered a loss in the process—because they sold their product at the asking price.

Other bot law

Here are a few other pieces of legislation that might be of interest to bot developers.

California Bot Disclosure Law: In 2018, California passed a law (Senate Bill 1001) that requires businesses to disclose the use of bots in online communications when the bot is used to interact with users in California. The law aims to provide transparency and protect consumers from being misled by automated accounts, particularly in sales or political contexts.

EU General Data Protection Regulation (GDPR): The GDPR, which took effect in 2018, is a comprehensive data protection regulation that covers various aspects of online privacy and security. While it doesn't specifically target bots, it does require transparency in data collection and processing, including automated decision-making and profiling. This can have implications for certain types of bots, particularly those that collect or process personal data.

Computer Fraud and Abuse Act (CFAA): The CFAA is a U.S. federal law that primarily targets computer crimes like hacking and unauthorized access to computer systems. While it doesn't specifically address bots, some legal experts argue that using bots to scrape websites or gain unauthorized access to information could potentially fall under the purview of the CFAA.

It's important to note that these laws and regulations often focus on specific types of bots or address particular issues related to their usage. The legal landscape surrounding bots is complex and evolving as new technologies and use cases emerge.

TRUE STORY: That day the FBI came calling

I mentioned earlier that I never ran into any real legal issues as a bot developer. But that's not to say I haven't had encounters with law enforcement. Before I get too far into this story, I should point out that my encounters with law enforcement were good ones. In fact, some were profitable. In the past, I have had law enforcement clients. I've even created automated policing software for the European Union. But the most memorable encounter was with the FBI. My FBI story goes like this.

A few years back, I sublet some extra office space to a friend. We mostly minded our own business during the week. But, we developed a tradition called "*Beer-Thirty*".

I'm not sure of the exact origin of Beer-Thirty, but I'm sure someone said something like "It's gotta be Beer-Thirty Somewhere", as in a reference to meaning they needed little encouragement to have a drink. This began a tradition of bringing a few bottles of interesting beer to work on Friday. And a few minutes after lunch, we'd tap the refrigerator and discuss our week while we drained a few beers. We would often be accompanied by an attorney, who had an office around the corner.

On one such Beer-Thirty, we were just wrapping-up when the office phone rang. The Caller ID was telling me that the call was coming from '*Cyber Security… blah, blah, blah*'. I assumed it was a recruiter as the office got a lot of those calls. I picked-up the phone and was greeted by an FBI Agent—not a recruiter, but a Federal Agent working for The FBI's *Cyber Security and Terrorism Task Force*. This was a special branch of the FBI set-up to deal primarily with terrorists. Not entirely prepared for doing anything other than walking home and sleeping off my happy hour, I wasn't sure what to say to this very specialized federal law enforcement officer. I think I asked if there was anything they needed. In turn, the Special Agent requested a meeting. We agreed to meet at my office the following Monday morning.

On Monday, two FBI agents appeared in my parking lot at the specific selected time. As I observed from my fourth floor window. I watched them—like two characters from Central Casting, emerging from their government issued, dark blue, four door, Ford Taurus. There was a young one, who said nothing, and an older, more experienced agent who did all the talking. I know these are all stereotypical descriptions, but they were sufficiently obvious that I didn't need to inquire as to which people were the FBI agents.

Not knowing what to expect. I met them at the elevator and welcomed the two FBI agents around the atrium and on to my office. After the prerequisite teas and coffees were offered, accepted, and distributed, we settled around my desk. Initially, we engaged in friendly banter, like, "Is that a photo of your kids?". That sort of thing.

This banter continued for at least twenty minutes when I finally said, "Do you mind me asking why you're here?"

The older agent—who was doing all the talking, responded simply by saying,

"We noticed that you speak at a lot of hacker conferences and you also spend a lot of time in Russia." We basically want to know who's in the neighborhood."

From a realistic standpoint, I suppose I always knew that The US State Department tracks who comes into, and goes out of, The United States based on the evidence we leave at Border Control. But how did they know I was spending much of my time in Moscow? I never once directly flew to, or from, Russia. All of my travel to the former Soviet Union emanated either from Madrid, Prague, or Amsterdam. Where all these countries co-operating? Was I on an INTERPOL watch list? Additionally, how did they know I go to "a lot of" hacker conferences? I did cover DEF CON 5, in Las Vegas, for Computer World Magazine in 1998, and I've done nine DEF CON talks since. But at some point you need to ask how much research the government does?

Fortunately for me, I couldn't do all that analysis so quickly in my head, but I did appreciate the reduced tension in the room lowered a lot after that. We continued to have a very interesting conversation. I talked about my experiences of being extorted by a criminal when I lead a group in Moscow. And, he told me what it's like to work in a government Terrorism Task Force.

At one point the agent leaned over my desk and asked, "Do clients ever ask you to do bad things?"

To which I paused and politely explained that it's a small community and reputation is everything. So, as such, no. But, I did ask him specifically what crimes his group is most interested in, and without hesitation he said terrorism and child pornography.

Years later I used the *FOIA*, or Freedom of Information Act, to obtain a copy of my FBI Dossier. I only suspected that I had an FBI Dossier because of the encounter I had with the Special Agent. My FBI Dossier did discuss my interview in detail. Though most of the document was redacted, I was able to discover that their involvement with me was far further reaching than what I could have imagined. There's much more to this story, but it's a matter for another book.

CHAPTER 15, DOM AND JAVASCRIPT

To fully understand how Selenium works, one must have an understanding of *DOM*—or the Document Object Model. This is because Selenium uses the Document Object Model almost exclusively to locate web objects (like text boxes, links, or page titles) on web pages.

The decision to include JavaScript in this chapter was made for several reasons. First, Selenium scripts bear more than a glancing resemblance to JavaScript functions. For example, Selenium's `driver.find_element(By.ID, '')` is very similar to JavaScript's, `document.findElementById('')`.

The second reason to include JavaScript here is the fact that Selenium can directly execute any JavaScript on the target page loaded by Webdriver. That's incredibly powerful, and alone makes JavaScript a valid topic for any Selenium developer.

If you're not familiar with JavaScript or DOM, don't be put off. The Document Object Model is fairly straight forward. Simply put, DOM represents a hierarchical description —an array actually, that relates to the structure, content, and style of web pages. It's presence is woven through the fabric of JavaScript, CSS, HTML, and therefore, most every web page your bots will encounter.

While I had programmed with JavaScript since its inception, I never felt accomplished at it until I started learning Selenium. This was wholly due to the fact I had to better understand DOM to use Selenium. And that new knowledge of the Document Object Model in turn led to more confidence while developing with JavaScript.

Knowledge of DOM is essential to understanding both how web elements are located by Selenium and also how to parse the contents of web pages. As such, you should consider this chapter a prerequisite to Chapter 18, *"Parsing text and the semantic web"*.

This following diagram illustrates the general structure of DOM.

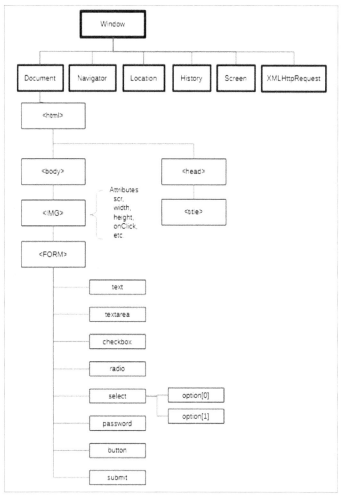

Figure 15.1, A simplified depiction of the Document Object Model

In the figure above, you can see the hierarchical nature of DOM, originating with the `window` object.

194

DOM objects

The Document Object Model is comprised of six major objects:

> Window,
>
> Navigator,
>
> Location,
>
> History,
>
> Screen, and
>
> XTMLHttpRequest.

Of the DOM objects, the object that you'll become most familiar within botDev is the Window Object, because that's where all the page content is. You probably won't use the other objects all that often. But it's important to know that they exist, because you will need all of them at some point.

The following is a detailed description of each of the Objects in the Document Object Model. If you already have a mastery of DOM, please feel free to skip to the last section on the history of DOM and JavaScript, which you'll see are very interrelated.

window.document

As mentioned earlier, the `window.document` object is where a web page's screen content is held. This includes, not only all the text, forms, images, but also all the HTML, CSS, and JavaScript that is included in the page. So this will be the object that any bot developer will become most familiar.

In JavaScript, the "`window.document`" object is usually just called "`document`". This is because JavaScript does unexpected things like default to the `window` object. The script below shows a simple web page with a form and a JavaScript function that reads the contents of two text boxes. Notice that while both text boxes live in the DOM, the script uses two different ways to locate them.

Shown below is a script that employs many aspects of the Document Object Model.

```
<document>
  <head>
    <script>

      function callOut()
        {
        /* find the element via its ID */
        var first = document.getElementById('id1');
        alert(first.value);

        /* find the element id2 via DOM */
        var second = document.forms[0].id2.value;
        alert(second);
        }

    </script>
  </head>
  <body>
    <form>
      <input type="text" value="Hello1" id="id1">
      <input type="text" value="Hello2" id="id2">
    </form>

    <script>
        callOut();
    </script>

  </body>
</document>
```

Script 15.1 An example using the document object.

In Script 15.1 above, the first line of JavaScript in `callOut()` should look familiar as it's very similar to Selenium's locator, `driver.find_element(By.ID)`. You will see more similarities between Selenium and JavaScript because each is very dependent on the Document Object Model.

window.location

The location property of the window object describes the location of the web page, or file, you're viewing in the browser. Notice here that JavaScript is not a precise language, as you can access the location property through either the window or document object, as shown in the script below. In practice, the location property is commonly accessed as

196

a member of the document object, which it technically isn't. But again, JavaScript is JavaScript.

```
<script>
  <!-- Show the current browser location, both of the following will work. ->
  alert(window.location)
  alert(document.location)

  <!-- Go to another website and page ->
  window.location="https://www.mepso.com/";

  <!--
    This will also work!
    document.location="https://www.mepso.com/";
  ->
```

Script 3.1.x, The exception to the rule: The location property.

window.navigator

JavaScript's `window.navigator` object in JavaScript provides information about the user's browser. It represents the browser's navigator or client-side environment and offers properties and methods to access various browser-related things. Here's an overview of the `window.navigator` object:

- User Agent Information
  - `navigator.userAgent` Returns the user agent string, which provides details about the browser, operating system, and other client information.
  - `navigator.appVersion` Returns the version of the browser application.
- Browser Identification
  - `navigator.vendor` Returns the browser vendor or company name.
  - `navigator.product` Returns the name of the browser's product, usually the same as the `navigator.vendor` value.
  - `navigator.platform` Returns the platform, or operating system, where the browser is running.
- Language and Localization
  - `navigator.language` Returns the preferred language of the user's browser.

- `navigator.languages` Returns an array of the user's preferred languages in order of preference.
- Geo-location
  - `navigator.geolocation` Provides access to the Geo-location API, allowing you to retrieve the user's current location if the user grants permission.
- Cookies and Storage
  - `navigator.cookieEnabled` Indicates whether cookies are enabled in the user's browser.
  - `navigator.onLine`: Indicates whether the browser is currently online or offline.
  - `navigator.storage` Provides access to the Storage API, which allows you to store data on the user's device.
- Media Capabilities
  - `navigator.mediaDevices` Provides access to media-related devices, such as cameras and microphones.
- Feature Detection
  - `navigator.userAgentData` Provides information about the browser's capabilities and features, including supported image and video formats, hardware support, and more.

The `navigator` object is commonly used for browser detection, feature detection, language localization, and accessing various browser-related information to customize the user experience or adapt functionality accordingly.

window.screen
In JavaScript, the `screen` object is directly accessed through the `window.screen` property. The `window.screen` object provides information about the user's screen or monitor, including its dimensions, color depth, pixel density, and other related properties. It is a part of the `window` object, which is the global object in the browser's JavaScript environment.

The `window.screen` is important for the following reasons:

- Responsive Web Design
    - With the `window.screen` object, you can retrieve the screen dimensions (`width` and `height`) to create responsive web designs. By adapting your layout and content based on the available screen space, you can ensure a better user experience across different devices and screen sizes.

- Media Queries
    - Media queries in CSS can use properties from the `window.screen` object, such as `width` or `resolution`, to apply specific styles or adjust the layout based on the user's screen properties. This allows for more targeted styling for different devices and resolutions.

- Device Detection
    - By accessing the `window.screen` object, you can gather information about the user's screen and device capabilities. This can be used for device detection or to apply different logic or functionality based on the user's screen size, pixel density, or other screen-related properties.

- Screen-Related Calculations
    - The `window.screen` object provides information that can be used for calculations or positioning elements on the screen. For example, you can determine the available screen space (`availWidth` and `availHeight`) to dynamically position elements or calculate proportions.

In summary, the `window.screen` object in JavaScript is significant for retrieving screen-related information and utilizing it for responsive web design, media queries, device detection, and screen-related calculations within your JavaScript code.

window.history
The window.history` object in JavaScript provides access to the browser's session history, allowing you to interact with the user's navigation history within a particular window or tab. Here's an overview of the `window.history` object:

- Navigation Methods

199

- history.back() Navigates the browser back to the previous page in the session history.
- history.forward() Navigates the browser forward to the next page in the session history.
- history.go(n) Navigates the browser to a specific page in the session history. The `n` parameter specifies the relative position in the history, where negative values represent going back and positive values represent going forward.

- Length
  - history.length Returns the number of entries in the session history for the current window or tab.
  - history.pushState(stateObj, title, url) Adds a new entry to the session history with the specified `stateObj`, `title`, and `url`. This does not trigger a page reload, and
  - history.replaceState(stateObj, title, url) Modifies the current entry in the session history with the specified `stateObj`, `title`, and `url`. This also does not trigger a page reload.

By utilizing the methods and properties of the window.history object, you can manipulate the browser's navigation history and handle the state changes triggered by the user's navigation actions. This allows you to create dynamic web applications that can navigate through history, update the URL without reloading the page, and manage application states.

It's also important to recognize that JavaSCript cannot read your browser history. This is important because otherwise, any website could figure out where you've browsed since the last time you cleared your browser history.

window.XMLHttpRequest
The `window.XMLHttpRequest` object, sometimes referred to as *XHR*, is a built-in JavaScript object that allows you to make HTTP requests from the browser. This technique, known as *AJAX* (Asynchronous JavaScript and XML), is widely used to create interactive web applications. It enables communication between the web page and

a server, after the web page has been downloaded. This active content must be triggered by some event, either caused by interaction with the person (or bot) viewing the web page, a timer, or some other process.

- Creating an XMLHttpRequest
  - `var newRequestObject = new XMLHttpRequest()` Creates a new instance of the `XMLHttpRequest` object.
- Making a Request
  - `xhr.open(method, url)` initializes a request with the specified HTTP `method` (e.g., "GET", "POST"), `url`.
  - `xhr.setRequestHeader(header, value)` : Sets the value of an HTTP request header before sending the request.
  - `xhr.send([data])` Sends the request to the server, optionally sending data in the request body.
- Handling the Response
  - `xhr.onreadystatechange` An event handler that is triggered whenever the `readyState` property of the `XMLHttpRequest` changes. You can use this to track the progress and handle the response.
  - `xhr.readyState` Represents the state of the request. It goes through different values as the request progresses, such as `0` (UNSENT), `1` (OPENED), `2` (HEADERS_RECEIVED), `3` (LOADING), and `4` (DONE).
  - `xhr.status` Returns the HTTP status code of the response (e.g., 200 for OK, 404 for Not Found).
- Event Listeners:
  - `xhr.onload` An event handler that is triggered when the request is successfully completed.
  - `xhr.onerror` An event handler that is triggered when an error occurs during the request.
  - `xhr.onprogress` An event handler that is triggered periodically to track the progress of the request.

○ `xhr.onloadend` An event handler that is triggered when the request completes, regardless of success or failure.

By utilizing the XMLHttpRequest object, web pages can retrieve data from a server, send data to a server, and update parts of a web page dynamically without requiring a full page reload.

A little history: DOM and JavaScript

JavaScript is essentially a DOM control language, but JavaScript actually preceded any formal definition of DOM by several years. JavaScript came into being in 1995 as Netscape wanted a client-side language that could provide interactivity to the early Web. So when Netscape 2.0 was released, it included the client-side language developed by *Brendan Eich*[17].

As you may know, JavaScript has little in common with Java, other than the fact that Netscape had a partnership with Sun Microsystems, who wanted a lighter client-side version of Java, so they co-opted the name. The new browser, and javascript, were greeted with immediate success.

When there was only one client-side web language there were obviously no compatibility problems. So JavaScript 1.0 was, and will always be, the only time there were no version compatibility issues with JavaScript.

But that situation was reversed when Microsoft introduced its own client-side language, *J-Script.* As a language, J-Script was *"nearly compatible"* with Netscape's JavaScript. As such, script compatibility issues were everywhere.

This mismatch of client-side scripting languages occurred amidst a period of rapid creativity, with new browser products being released one after another. As a result, many websites were thrown together using scripts that were compatible with either J-Script or JavaScript, but seldom both. Banners declaring "Best when Seen in Netscape 3.0" or

---

17   *JavaScript 1.0.* (2023, March 13). Web Design Museum. https://www.webdesignmuseum.org/web-design-history/javascript-1-0-1995

"This Website Requires Explorer 4.0" became far more common they they should have been.

So, unlike today, developers could not use client-side scripting for mission critical tasks[18]. Web developers of the time mostly relegated JavaScript (and to a lesser degree, J-Script) to providing decorative accouterments like scrolling text, image roll-overs[19]. And even then, there needed to be a focus on how to "fail gracefully" when a JavaScript compatibility issue erupted.

Another factor that exacerbated the compatibility issue was people's reluctance to upgrade their browsers. Many users stuck with the default browser that came installed on their computers, leading to modern web pages being accessed with decade-old browsers. This persistence of old versions of JavaScript and J-Script created a persistent problem that seemed to linger despite the passing of time.

This incompatibility frustrated many long-time developers, including myself. Although I needed to use JavaScript over the years, it was only recently that I came to terms with the problems the language caused during its early years..

To address the challenge of cross-compatibility among the various JavaScript versions, several measures were taken. The arrival of JQuery proved to be one of the most practical solutions, as it "programmed around" the shortcomings of the different incompatible versions of JavaScript.

DOM Level 1
In 1998, the *World Wide Web Consortium, or* W3C, introduced DOM Level 1 as a standardized API, or Application Programming Interface, for accessing and manipulating HTML and XML documents. It defined a set of objects, methods, and properties that allowed developers to interact with the structure, content, and style of web pages programmatically. DOM Level 1 formed the foundation of modern DOM implementations.

---

18 For the sake of discussion, a "mission cs

19 Schrenk, M. (n.d.). The Michael Schrenk javascript animation tutorial. http://schrenk.com/js/

DOM Level 2

By 2000, DOM Level 2 expanded on the capabilities of DOM Level 1. It introduced new features, including support for XML namespaces, event handling, and CSS (Cascading Style Sheets) manipulation. It also provided mechanisms for traversing and manipulating the DOM tree more efficiently. DOM Level 2 was released in three separate modules: Core, Events, and Style.

DOM Level 3

Between 2004 and 2010, DOM Level 3 further extended the functionality of the DOM. It introduced additional features such as support for XPATH (a language for navigating XML documents), better event handling, and improved error handling. DOM Level 3 was also released in multiple modules, including Core, Events, Load and Save, Validation, and Views.

DOM4

In 2015, DOM4 was a minor update that aimed to clarify and refine certain aspects of the DOM specification. It addressed issues identified in earlier versions and provided better consistency and interoperability across different browsers.

The Living Standard:

Starting in 2016, the DOM specification transitioned to a "Living Standard" maintained by the WHATWG (Web Hypertext Application Technology Working Group). This approach allows for continuous evolution and improvement of the DOM specification to keep up with the ever-changing web landscape. The Living Standard is implemented by modern web browsers.

Since the Living Standard, the DOM has continued to evolve through ongoing updates and refinements to meet the demands of new web technologies and standards.

Overall, the DOM has played a crucial role in enabling dynamic and interactive web experiences by providing a standardized interface for accessing and manipulating web page content programmatically.

CHAPTER 16, SELENIUM LOCATORS

We used locators in Section II without much fanfare. So, this is a good time to look more deeply into Selenium's ability to find and interact with web page objects. If you haven't already done so, it is highly recommended that you read the previous chapter on DOM and how it is integrated into Selenium.

The important thing to remember is that Selenium works, largely, by identifying page objects through the DOM and then interacting with that element through Webdriver. This section focuses on the `find_element` object, how it locates objects, and how it interacts with the objects it identifies.

find_element object

The primary way Selenium Python accesses the DOM is through `find_element`. Script 16.1, shows the various methods Selenium uses to locate objects on a web page.

```
# Locators
driver.find_element(By.ID, "id")
driver.find_element(By.NAME, "name")
driver.find_element(By.LINK_TEXT, "link text")
driver.find_element(By.PARTIAL_LINK_TEXT, "partial link text")
driver.find_element(By.XPATH, "xpath")
driver.find_element(By.TAG_NAME, "tag name")
driver.find_element(By.CLASS_NAME, "class name")
driver.find_element(By.CSS_SELECTOR, "css selector")
```

Script 16.1, the six ways Selenium identifies objects on web pages

The figure above shows the valid identifier types Selenium uses to find objects on web pages. Each method interacts with the DOM at one level or another. Why are there so many ways to address DOM objects? Because the locators are not always readily available. If your remember, the procurement bot demonstration in Section II came across a submit button with no identifier whatsoever.

It should be noted that `find_element` is unique to Selenium Python. Other flavors of Selenium may use other commands. For example, the find_element equivalent in Selenium Java is `findElement`.

Let's look at how each of these identifier types are used.

Finding elements by names and IDs

Identifying DOM objects by their name or ID is as easy as using the ID or name that the web objects were assigned, as shown in Script 16.2 below.

```
# Example HTML
<body>
    <div id="div1">1995</div>
    <div name="div2">2014</div>
</body>
```

Script 16.2, Assigning ID and name identifiers in HTML

The script above shows how names and IDs are assigned to objects, this case a pair of `<div>` tags.

The script below, in Script 16.3, shows how the contents of these containers are read by Selenium Python.

```
# Selenium Python to retrieve the contents from the above DIV sections
data1 = driver.find_element(By.ID, "div1").innerHTML
data2 = driver.find_element(By.NAME, "div2").innerHTML
```

Script 16.3, Selenium, used to capture the contents of two DIV containers

The script above assigns the contents of two div containers into two Python variables. Each assignment shows how the content of two `DIV` sections are retrieved. In each case the `find_element` is used. In one case to locate an `ID` and in the other, to locate a NAME. In both cases, the `DIV` content was found in the innerHTML attribute.

206

Similarities between Selenium and JavaScript

Again, you may notice stark similarities between Selenium Python and JavaScript. This is because both languages are dependent on the DOM to locate things on web pages. For example, compare and contrast the two following scripts.

```
# SELENIUM PYTHON CODE
data1 = driver.find_element(By.ID, "div1").innerHTML
```

Script 16.4, Obtaining the contents of a DIV section with Selenium Python

```
# JAVASCRIPT CODE
data1 = document.getElementById("DIV1").innerHTML;
```

Script 16.5, Obtaining the contents of a DIV section with

Both of the scripts above read the contents of a DIV section, one with Selenium Python and the other with JavaScript. These lines of code are similar because they each use the Document Object Model, and there are only so many ways to label the same things.

Selenium isn't limited to reading the attributes of web objects. It can also set those attributes to specific values and execute any available methods, as shown in the code snippet that follows.

```
# Write value to DIV container
driver.find_element_by_id("div1").click()            # click on object
driver.find_element_by_id("div1").send_keys("hello")  # write to object
```

Script 16.5, Selenium can write to DOM attributes and execute available methods

The point of this section is to show that `find_element` can be used to locate object for either reading or writing.

Locating and clicking on links

Selenium Python allows developers to find links either by identifying the link's link text, or partial link text, as shown in the following script.

```
'''
HTML
<a href="https://www.google.com">Go to Google.</a>
'''
```

```
# Either of the following Selenium Python statements will click the link described above
driver.find_element(By.LINK_TEXT, "Go to Google").click()
driver.find_element(By.PATIAL_LINK_TEXT, "Google").click()
```

Script 16.6, Selenium Python clicking on full and partial links

In the code above, the link is first identified and then clicked. If more than on condition is satisfied—or if there were more than one link meets the criteria of the partial link, Selenium will return an array of objects that fit the description. You will then have to select which of the objects in the array you want to act on. This doesn't happen very often, but it does happen with some frequency when Selenium is looking for objects using CSS, TAG or CLASS identifiers.

Locating elements by XPATH

Not every item on a web page has an assigned name, ID, or link text. So how are these items identified? In these cases, my preference is to use XPATH.

XPATH, or XML Path Language, is a query language used to navigate and select elements within an XML or HTML document. It provides a way to traverse the document's hierarchical structure and identify specific nodes based on their relationships, attributes, or content. XPATH expressions are written as paths that describe the location of elements relative to the document's root or other reference points. It is commonly used in web scraping and automation testing, particularly with tools like Selenium, to locate and interact with elements on web pages by defining their unique paths within the

208

HTML structure. XPATH is powerful and flexible, allowing precise selection of elements, making it a valuable tool for working with XML and HTML documents.

```
#######################
# HTML EXAMPLE
#---------------------
<html>
    <body>
        <table>
            <tr>
                <td>ONE</td>
                <td>TWO</td>
            </tr>
            <tr>
                <td>THREE</td>
                <td>FOUR</td>
            </tr>
            <tr>
                <td>FIVE</td>
                <td>SIX</td>
            </tr>
        </table>
    </body>
</html>


#######################
# XPATH REPRESENTATIONS
#---------------------
xpath = "/html/body/table/tr[2]/td/body>"       # contains "TWO"
xpath = "/html/body/table/tr[3]/td[2]/body>"    # contains "SIX"
```

Script 16.7, Resolving XPATH designations

In the example in Script 16.7, the string that defines the XPATH (and it's always a string) for the table cell that contains the text "TWO" is defined. XPATH starts at the top level of DOM and works it's way down to the desired object. If we wanted to say what this XPATH is saying we might say something like,

> *"Within HTML document, and then within the BODY, and then within the first TABLE, and then within the Second Row (XPATH indexes always start with one), and within that table cell."*

The things to remember about XPATH:

1. XPATH is hierarchical and follows the Document Object Model, and

2. XPATH uses indexed arrays to describe when there are multiple objects of the same type and DOM level.

While this XPATH example was simple most are not. Web pages may have thousands of objects on them, so writing your own XPATH by hand is tedious and error prone. To get accurate XPATH descriptions, it's best to use a tool like Chrome Inspect, which is described in Chapter 23.

Limitations of using XPATH

One limitation of XPATH is that it is position dependent—not within the web page, but within the DOM. If in the previous example, a table was added before the targeted table, the XPATH would fail because it was no long in the same location in the DOM. At the very least, developers will want to use Python's exception handling to ensure fault tolerance to web page changes. Chapter 20, Fault Tolerance, addresses this topic in greater detail.

Locating elements by tag names

Another option when locating web page objects is to reference them by TAG_NAME. The `find_element(By.TAG_NAME, 'tag name')` function returns the first matching web element found on the page that corresponds to the specified HTML tag name. If there are multiple elements with the same tag name, it will return an array of matches.

If you want to return all tags that match a description, use the find_elements (notice the plural) function.

```
'''
Example HTML
<body>
    <img src="image1.png">
    <img src="image2.png">
</body>
'''

# Selenium Python code to find the first image
firstImg = driver.find_element(By.TAG_NAME, "img")

# Selenium Python using find_element(s)
ARRImg = driver.find_elements(By.TAG_NAME, "img")
firstImg = ARRImg[0]
secondImg = ARRImg[1]
```

Script 16.8, Using the find_element() & find_elements() functions

You will find similar circumstances. When more than one item matches the locator, anticipate that only the first result is returned, unless other measures are taken, as was done above in Script 16.8.

Locating elements by style

Another option is to load elements based on their (CSS) Class Name or by a CSS Selector.

```
obj1 = driver.find_element(By.CLASS_NAME, "class name")
obj2 = driver.find_element(By.CSS_SELECTOR, "css selector")
```

Script 16.9, finding web objects by class designations

As in previous examples, find_element(By.CLASS_NAME, "classname") will return the first item it finds in the DOM tree that was assigned that specific class name.

By contrast, the statement, `find_element(By.CLASS_NAME, `*classname*`)`, matches objects with CSS selectors. If you've forgotten, here is a quick review of CSS selectors.

```
```
<html>
    <head>
        styles
            {
            p.center{text-align:center; color:red;}
            }
    </head>
    <body>
        <p class="center">red and centered.</p>
    </body>
</html>
```

obj = driver.find_element(By.CSS_Selector, "p.center")
```

Script 16.10, Using find_element(By.CSS_Selector)

Searching for page elements by CSS selector can be very exclusive. It is very handy for selecting (clicking on) specific items in highly stylized select lists or other custom web controls.

212

CHAPTER 17, WEBDRIVER

Webdriver is the generic term for Selenium's interface to the browser. Webdriver provides direct read/write access to anything that's happening in a variety of browsers. We access Webdriver through Selenium—primarily with the `find_element` and `get` methods, via Python.

Differences between Webdrivers

There are a variety of Webdrivers supported by Selenium, to match the desired browser environment. While the list is smaller than it might have been twenty years ago, the list still includes most of the browsers you might need to emulate—either for compatibility with a website, or to test browser incompatibilities.

The current list of supported browsers includes:

- Chrome (ChromeDriver),

- Firefox (GeckoDriver),

- Microsoft Edge (EdgeDriver),

- Apple's Safari (SafariDriver), and

- Opera (OperaDriver)

This book defaults all selection of Webdriver to Chromedriver. This was a deliberate choice made for the following reasons:

1. The various versions of Webdriver are controlled the same way and should be plug-and-play compatible with whatever working Selenium Python script your already have,

2. By focusing on one Webdriver a lot of repetition was avoided and opportunities to focus on "Webdriver" as a topic, and not a specific piece of software, and finally,

3. The final decision to focus exclusively on Chrome was due to it's widespread use and the perceived superiority of the Chrome Inspect tool, which is discussed in Chapter 23.

Any distinctions you find between versions of Webdriver should be minimal. The main distinction for most bot developers may be differences in the JavaScript engines, though differences should be slight considering the amount of code that is shared among the versions.

The primary advantage to defining the browser environment with the Webdriver is that your bots can spoof any browser by simply loading a different Webdriver. In other words, you can pick the name of the browser that is inserted into the server logs when your bot accesses a server. This is particularly useful among test engineers, who may write regression tests[20] that check for browser compatibility issues.

Another—and almost as successful, way to spoof a browser is by editing the *Agent Name*, or the identifier your browser uses to identify itself, in the Webdriver options when the Webdriver is loaded. This allows Chromedriver, for example, to spoof any browser ever made. The options list also allows for setting screen size, and other browser parameters that indicate that the bot is emulating a mobile device, etc. The limitations of spoofing an agent name is that you lack the specific rendering and JavaScript engines you're attempting to emulate.

Matching versions: Webdriver and your browser

When using Chromedriver, for example, it's essential to ensure that both Chrome and the WebDriver have matching revision levels. This is one of the first areas of confusion that a new Selenium Python developer is likely to experience. One day your bot is running fine. The next day your bot can't load Webdriver because of a version conflict. This happens when your browser automatically updates itself to the current version while the Webdriver remains outdated. And while auto updates might be good for end users, they're awful for bot developers because the browser version changes every few weeks.

---

20   Regression testing was addressed with the bot example in Section II, Project 7.

I have made many failed attempts to turn-off auto updates in Chrome. Some of the steps I've taken to stop auto updates include: Removing the scheduled tasks that check for browser updates, renaming the directory where the Chrome update code resides, and finally I have deleted that said directory. Nothing I have tried has kept Chrome from auto updating. Perhaps you'll have better luck.

Typically, I will keep one (current) copy of Webdriver in my development file structure, and all bots use this same copy of the software. While this doesn't eliminate the problem, it does simplify maintenance.

The Webdriver protocol

The Webdriver protocol is a standard developed by the World Wide Web Consortium (W3C) that defines a way for testing web applications by automating browsers. Webdriver provides a platform, and a language-neutral protocol, as a way for programs to control web browsers, much like a person would manually.

Figure 17.1, Webdriver's relationship to Selenium Python control and information flow

The Webdriver protocol consists of a set of commands that can be sent to a browser--or more accurately, a Webdriver compatible driver like ChromeDriver. These commands allow for a variety of interactions with the browser, such as navigating to a new URL, clicking elements on the page, or retrieving the current page source.

When a Selenium Python program issues the command to "get" a web page or to "find_element", those commands are ultimately sent from Selenium to Webdriver via an HTTP connection. Using HTTP in this way, and using a defined protocol, allows for a large degree of language independence.

The Webdriver protocol is the underlying technology that allows Selenium (and similar tools) to interact with web browsers. By providing a standard set of commands and responses, it allows for a wide variety of automation tasks to be performed in a consistent way across different browsers and platforms.

Webdriver at a glance

Here are a few things to remember about Webdriver.

Webdriver is the generic term for Selenium's interface to web browsers, providing direct read/write access to browsers and browser interactions.

With Selenium Python, Python indirectly controls web pages by controlling Selenium, which interfaces to Webdriver via the Webdriver protocol.

There are versions of Webdriver to match most browser environments, including Chrome, Firefox, Microsoft Edge, and Apple's Safari. This book defaults to using Chromedriver for simplicity.

It's crucial to ensure that the Webdriver version and your browser's revision level match to avoid version conflicts. Auto-updates in browsers can lead to compatibility issues, so keeping a consistent Webdriver version can help mitigate these problems.

Chapter 18, Parsing text and the semantic web

Parsing text can be one of the most daunting tasks a developer can tackle. But that job can be made easier if a few techniques and a small library are applied. This chapter compresses over twenty years of parsing experience into a few pages.

What is parsing?

The word *parsing* has several definitions in devOps. The oldest definition of a parser was a piece of software that parsed, and interpreted the meaning of computer source code. This is a process performed by every computer language. Interpreted languages like PHP parse the source code before every execution. While compiled languages build a byte-code version of the program from the parsed source code.

Our use and definition of parsing is a little simpler than that used in computer languages. And, these are the situations our parsing tools are tuned for. All we want to do is separate data that we want from text and scripts that we don't want. This often involves separating data from it's format. Other times, it's a matter of directly reading variables from HTML, JavaScript, or from reading GET/POST variables.

Additionally, the data that bots parse is often periodic in that it appears in repeating HTML tags that have a given structure. Or the data exists in formatted data tables. And sometimes, when our bots get really lucky, the data us nicely formatted in XML or JSON formats.

How my parsing techniques evolved

When I started bot development in the mid '90s, there were only a few commonly used "web aware" languages to pick from. The two that were most commonly used at the time were, Java, and PHP.

One of the things that drew me to PHP was its ability to manipulate strings. As a result, I found a few aspects of Python lacking when I learned the language. Things that I took for granted in PHP were either missing or noticeably hard to use in Python.

I was fortunate in that my parsing strategies were solidified early on. The main advantage to having a strategy (and a library) is that parsing tasks can be completed much faster and with higher reliability.

Screen scraper focused parsing

The ability to parse text is fundamental to writing bots, particularly screen scrapers. Many people are turned off by the prospect of decoding useful information from arbitrary text. And much of the reason for this is there are a lot of ways to manipulate text (strings) in most languages. Parsing is one case where it pays to think ahead and to develop some strategy before one starts.

Developing a parsing strategy

One of the problems in developing a parsing strategy is that modern languages offer many ways to manipulate strings. It can be daunting. Where do you start? There are two main strategies that have severed me well for over twenty-five years. My parsing strategy basically boils down to:

ProTip!

1. Limiting your set of go-to tools to just a few, and

2. Building *"wrapper functions"* that hide the complexity of what the function is doing.

The four most used parsing functions (libParse.py)

If you've read other things I've written, you may recognize both my parsing style as well as the functions I use to parse. These functions first made their appearance in the first edition of "Webbots, Spiders, and Screen Scrapers". In that series of books, a parsing library named LIB_parse.php was put into the public domain and used heavily. Now that my attention has shifted to Python, that library has been rewritten as libParse.py. The core parsing functions from that library, first published in 2007, make up the core of the

218

Python library. So these routines have lasted the test of two books and nearly twenty-five years of use!

The following functions are found in libParse.py I have been using these algorithms for literally decades and they still prove useful.

stringOut splitString(stringIn, splitText, BEFORE/AFTER)

The most basic task in parsing is being able to split a string at a given point within that string. This function, splitString() facilitates splitting strings with the use of the following parameters:

Parameter	Description
stringOut	This is the output string, essentially a substring of the inputString, split before, or after, the splitText.
stringIn	The subject string
splitText	The delineation point where stringIn is split.
BEFORE/AFTER	The BEFORE and AFTER constants are used to denote which side of the string is desired.

Figure 18.1, The interface to splitString()

The splitString() function is one of those glue tools. It will never be a major part of your parses, but it is one of the handier functions.

```
'''
USE CASES
'''

# Parse the head of the HTML page (where html = HTML page contents)
headTxt = splitString(html, "<BODY", BEFORE)

# Parse the text from an ordered list
bulletTxt = "<li>This is bullet point three
thirdBulletTxt = splitString(bulletTxt, "<li>", AFTER)
```

Script 18.1, Examples of using splitString()

String splitting functions enable the extraction of distinct parts or segments from a given string. In scenarios involving disorganized or unstructured data, employing string splitting aids in the cleansing and arrangement of information. By eliminating redundant characters, spaces, or separators, a more uniform dataset is established. This is particularly effective when used in an iterative loop.

Moreover, string splitting proves valuable in the dissection of URLs, facilitating the extraction of diverse elements like protocol, domain, path, and query parameters. This is particularly useful in activities such as web scraping and the development of web applications. Notably, when handling extensive datasets, the division of strings tends to be more efficient than manual manipulation, particularly when confronting repetitive or intricate patterns.

stringParsed = returnBetween(stringIn, begTag, endTag, INCL/EXCL)
One of the most useful parsing tools is the ability to extract text between two landmarks (in this case called `begTag` and `endTag`). The function `returnBetween()` has the following interface:

Parameter	Description
stringParsed	This is the output string, essentially a substring of the inputString, that exists between begTag and endTag,
stringIn	The subject string
begTag, endTag	The begin tag and end tag mark the delineation points where your desired text begins and ends. Your target text should be between these parameters.
INCL/EXCL	Use INCL if you'd like the begin/end delineation marks returned in stringOut, or use EXCL if you'd like them excluded. It is sometimes useful to include the delineation marks while debugging your parsing scripts.

Figure 18.2, The interface to returnBetween()

The `returnBetween()` function is one of my bread-and-butter tools. I use it to parse XML, json, or any case where the data you want is encased between landmarks.

220

Some examples follow in Script 18.2.

```
'''
USE CASES returnBetween()
'''
# Get an attribute from a HTML tag
tagTxt = "<a href="http://www.google.com">Google</a>"
urlTXT = returnBetween(tagTxt, 'href="', '"', EXCL)

# Parse the text between HTML tags (where html contains the web page).
titleTxt = returnBetween(html, "<title>", "</title>", EXCL)   # returns title, minus tags

# Parse the XML
xmlStr   = returnBetween(html, "<XML", "</XML>", INCL)         # returns XML, incl XML tags
xmlTxt   = returnBetween(xmlStr, "<DATE>", "</DATE>", EXCL)    # returns DATE from XML tags
```

Script 18.2, Examples of using returnBetween()

There are a couple of points of note when using the `returnBetween()` function. If your begin tag is an HTML tag, you might not want to close the tag. This is because many HTML tags have attributes that are apt to change from web page to web page. That's why the "<XML" tag cited above isn't closed but the "`<title>`" tag is.

In cases like parsing the titleTxt, above, it's usually better to exclude the beginning and ending tags in the returned string. But, in a situation like parsing the XML, the beginning and end tags are included. Often, the INCL directive is used if you're having problems and need to debug parsing scripts.

arrayOut parseArray(stringIn, begTag, endTag)

The HTML that bots parse is often full of data that is encased in repeating patterns. For example, HTML tags that define, images, tables, divs, links, and iframes, are just a few examples. The function parseArray() returns an array (Python list) of data defined by the following interface:

Parameter	Description
arrayOut	This is the array (Python list) that is defined by the input parameters
stringIn	The subject string, in botDev, often a web page.
begTag, endTag	These are the delimiters that our data exists within. These often represent bookended <td></td>" tags, <a>

Figure 18.3 The parseArray() function interface

The `parseArray()` function is ideal for extracting repeating patterns, like parsing image files in Script 18.3 below.

```
'''
parseArray() and returnBetween() are often used together
in an iterative loop, as shown below
'''

# Get all the images from a web page (in the var html)
arrImgTags = parseArray(html, '<img', '>', INCL)          # Create array of image tags

# Now use returnBetween() to parse the actual image value
for imgTag in arrImgTags:
    image = libParse.returnBetween(imgTag, 'src="', '"', EXCL)
    print(image)
```

Script 18.3, Examples of using parseArray()

As shown above, the parseArray() and returnBetween() functions are often used together. If I were to make an educated guess, I'd wager that—combined, these two functions can parse 80% of your parsing needs.

This function is what I call a wrapper function or a function that is designed to either simplify the interface, or make the interface fulfill a standard. In reality, if you look at

222

the code, the `parseArray()` function uses a python regular expression to do the parse. Like most regEx commands, it's ugly and not very memorable. It's better to mask this ugliness when possible.

bool = stristr(stringHaystack, stringNeedle)

An example of a wrapper function that was don't to conform to standards is `libParse.stristr()`. This function is designed to resemble the same function in the PHP parsing library I placed into the Public Domain when my first bot book was published in 2007. Simply put, this function returns True when a substring appears in a string. This function is often used to validate landmarks.def trim(string):

```
trimmed = string.strip()
return trimmed
```

Script 18.4, Implementing the PHP stristr() in Python

Why libParse and not Beautiful Soup?

This book employs libParse.py, a python version of the PHP parsing library, LIB_parse.php that I published as an open source resource when my first Bot book was published in 2007. Many of you with Python backgrounds may ask, "Why aren't we using Beautiful Soup, the popular Python parsing library?"

If you like, and are familiar with Beautiful Soup, I encourage you to use what's familiar. And for those of you who are not familiar with Beautiful Soup, please check it out.

Beautiful Soup is essentially a DOM reader. You tell it where to look within the DOM, and Beautiful Soup will find it for you. For example, compare how Beautiful Soup retrieves the Title of a webpage, below.

```
# Get the page title with Beautiful Soup
soup = BeautifulSoup(html_doc, 'html.parser')
title = (soup.title.text)

# Get the page title with libParse
title = returnBetween(html, "<title>", "</title>", EXCL)
```

Script 18.5, Parsing a web pate title, BeautifulSoup v. LibParse

Selecting landmarks

Some of the things to consider when selecting a landmark include the following:

Specificity

Choose a landmark that is unique and specific to the target page, making it less likely for the bot to confuse it with similar elements on other pages. Part of this decision is the length of your landmark string. The longer strings will be more unique in the long run. Shorter strings are less definite but a lot more convenient.

Consistency

Select a landmark that is unlikely to change frequently. Elements that are part of the website's layout or core structure are typically more stable than those that may change due to content updates or dynamic elements. Some of the best landmarks, at least for stability reasons, include those page elements that are common with server functions. For example, page elements that refer to $_GET and $_POST methods tend to be really stable because these variables are written into server code, which is less likely to change than a styling update.

Accessibility

Ensure that the chosen landmark is easily accessible through the DOM (Document Object Model) and can be consistently identified using standard selectors, such as IDs, class names, or other attributes.

Relevance

The landmark should be relevant to the bot's intended tasks or actions on the page. For example, if the bot is designed to interact with a specific form, a suitable landmark would be an element associated with that form.

Visibility

Ideally, the landmark should be visible to users and not hidden or obscured by CSS styles or other elements. This ensures that the bot is comparing elements that are actually present on the page as perceived by users.

Availability

Consider the load time of the landmark element. If the element takes time to load or is rendered through JavaScript, the bot may need to incorporate additional logic, such as waiting for the element to appear or monitoring for changes in the DOM.

Tolerance to change

Websites may undergo redesigns or updates that change the source code. Choose a landmark that is less likely to be affected by these changes or can be easily adapted to accommodate them.

By considering these factors, a bot can select an appropriate landmark that helps ensure accurate and reliable identification of the target page, minimizing the risk of errors or unexpected behavior during its operation.

The Semantic Web

The Semantic web is worth a mention here because it's promise, and subsequent failure, is what eventually lead to DOM and the fact that websites are so difficult to parse.

What does "semantic" mean?

In computer science and web development, the term "semantic" refers to the practice of using meaningful and descriptive markup to represent the content and structure of web pages. Semantic HTML involves the use of specific HTML elements that carry significant information about their content. This approach makes it easier for both machines, such as search engines, and people, including users with disabilities, to understand the page's structure and content.

For instance, rather than using generic `<div>` tags, employing appropriate HTML elements like `<h1>`, `<nav>`, `<article>`, and `<footer>` provides semantic meaning to the different sections of a web page. This improved structure enhances the overall accessibility and interpretation of the content by various systems and users.

You may know Tim Berners-Lee as the British computer scientist, widely known as the inventor of the World Wide Web. He also recognized that while the web was growing rapidly, it lacked a structured and semantic understanding of the information it contained. He envisioned a web where data could be linked, interpreted, and understood by machines, enabling more intelligent interactions and automated processing. This vision led to the concept of the Semantic Web.

A bot-friendly environment

What Berners-Lee was suggesting was a very bot-friendly environment. His concept for a semantic web meant that the formatting of a webpage—which is almost never of use to bot developers, would be completely separate from the content. And, the content would essentially be "tagged" to identify its contents. Think of something that would look like inline XML in webpages.

Current status

The Semantic Web is an ongoing and evolving endeavor, and its full realization is still a work in progress. While significant advancements have been made in terms of technologies, standards, and adoption, the Semantic Web is not yet fully pervasive across the entire web.

The Semantic Web still faces challenges and limitations. These include scalability concerns, complexity in creating and maintaining ontologies, data quality issues, and the need for increased adoption and awareness among developers and organizations. There are ongoing research efforts to address these challenges and explore new approaches.

Reasons why the semantic web never really happened

While the Semantic Web has made significant advancements, there have been challenges and limitations that have hindered its widespread adoption and realization. Some of the notable failures or obstacles associated with the Semantic Web include: complexity, lack of awareness, and problems in annotating the data.

But the real reason that the semantic web faces resistance of is that there are few incentives for an organization to develop websites semantically. HTML and unstructured content, have been working just fine. And, most websites don't need this level of interoperability.

CHAPTER 19, SCALING AND ARCHITECTURE

The problem with scaling bots is that they are often too efficient for their own good. The fact is that it's easy to develop a bot that works too aggressively, especially in the fever of an exciting new project. This aggression is defined as a bot that accesses its target website more often that is required by the project. And from the projects I've worked on, most bots could access their sources less frequently and not miss any performance goals.

When a bot accesses a source too often, it will consume both excessive network bandwidth and server CPU cycles. This is when you enter the problems of Trespass to Chattel as described in Chapter 14.

The reality is that it is really easy to inadvertently overpower a network because today, even small computers have a lot of power. For that matter, old computers had this capacity too. Even an old, early '90s, 33MHz, IBM PC had enough power to completely flood a full T1 line. Imagine what your bot (or parallel bots) could do on modern equipment.

The problem with scaling

Before you start to scale your bot project to mammoth proportions, it's worth reviewing that often, you can't scale the output of your bot without also needing to scale the output of our source. The following story should be a warning to anyone, who thinks they can scale any bot to any capacity.

My experiences with over-eager bots

Many years ago I was developing a bot for one of my better clients. This project involved scraping recent court records. Once I had successfully set up the bot, it began collecting records at a pace that appeared entirely reasonable. And when I say "reasonable," I mean it operated at a speed and pattern that mimicked an actual person performing the mundane task of retrieving court records—something that likely occurs frequently.

My first mistake is that I started my collection on a Saturday, and not during the week when my bot's traffic would be mixed with regular traffic. Instead, the server logs left by my bot would be left while few others were using the system, making my logs more significant than they would be if mixed with hoards of other traffic.

The second mistake I made was in scaling. I calculated how much data I was collecting per minute and concluded that I would not be able collect everything by my Monday deadline. So, I opened things up. In stead of requesting data at a reasonable rate, I decided to collect as quickly as I could. Basically, the only things that restricted how fast the bot collected data was the speed of the computers and a little network lag.

Initially, my scaled-up, accelerated bot worked fine. I was collecting data at a break neck pace. Satisfied with what I had done, I left the bot to run autonomously, while I did something else.

After a short break, I came back to the bot. It had stopped running, and I assumed that it had completed it's collection. What I found instead is that the bot had failed and exited prematurely. To my surprise, pages were getting downloaded, but nothing was getting parsed correctly. I next turned to a copy of the last page the bot had downloaded (it's always a good idea to save files to disk). To my shock the web page had changed from a directory of court filings to something a tad more threatening. That message is paraphrased on the next page.

> ## You have reached the ### Court System for the State of ###.
>
> You are in gross violation of the user agreement.
>
> We have recorded and blocked your IP address.
>
> Please contact us at 555-555-5555 during regular business hours to address your next steps.

Figure 19.1, Message my bot received from a State Court system

I think my heart skipped a beat when I saw that message. Again, I was still early in my bot development career, but I was at it long enough to know that I had screwed-up terribly. Additionally, I was in trouble with a State's Court System, and if that meant anything, it meant they had more lawyers at their disposal than I had…!

I had to call the number provided the first thing on Monday morning. I also decided that I was not going to deny anything and tell them exactly what I was doing. Since this event happened on a Saturday morning, I had all weekend to ponder the consequences of my— or my bot's, actions.

When Monday came, I called the number and got an over-worked IT help desk person on the line. Without having to explain myself, they acknowledged that I was accessing their system too fast, and to access records at a more reasonable rate in the future. Expecting a more confrontational conversation, I politely thanked them and hung-up.

The only other time I ran afoul with a bot was, incidentally, for the same client. In that case I was monitoring some products that were appearing at an auction. Auction items were added a few an hour, but my client wanted to be the first to know when a new item was available for purchase. So, I was commissioned to write a bot that scanned the available auction items. When a new item was listed, my bot displayed the details of the sale. And to get my client's attention, the quick bark of a small dog would sound.

Since you're reading about this now, you can guess that I was scanning the auction site way too quickly. Quickly enough to receive a phone call from the IT guy running the auction site. Again, this was going to be a critical phone call because this was a very important procurement source for my client. And they weren't paying me to make their business more difficult to conduct.

I got on that phone call and was able to convince the manager on the other end of the line that we were actually a better customer because of our bot because it allowed us to buy more product from them. Secondly, I promised to scan their web pages more conservatively in the future.

I didn't have a lot of time to think about what I was going to say. And as soon as I said my piece I realized how frivolous my excuse sounded. Mine was a silly argument because we weren't actually helping them sell more product. If we hadn't found and purchased underpriced merchandise on their website, someone else would have. The reality was we were cherry picking their inventory.

The intent of recalling those two memories is to demonstrate that it is easy to run bots 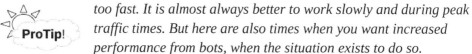 *too fast. It is almost always better to work slowly and during peak traffic times. But here are also times when you want increased performance from bots, when the situation exists to do so.*

The trick to scaling a bot is to add capacity while not producing too much strain on the target websites you use as sources. In other words, performance and long-term viability are two of the factors bot developers must consider when deciding if it is even a good idea to make the bot run faster.

If your bot is limited to one public data source, your limitation as to how fast your bot(s) can run is not based on technical abilities, but rather on how friendly you want to be to your source.

Now that you've been warned about the dangers of over-scaling, the rest of this chapter focuses on various bot architectures and where and how they are used.

Standalone bot architectures

The simplest bot architecture is the standalone architecture, where the bot is fully self contained, stores data locally, and doesn't support remote control. Each of the example bot projects in Section II are like the standalone bot depicted in the figure below. The exception is the bot in the parsing exercises in Section II, Project 6. While this architecture is useful, it also has limitations, as follows.

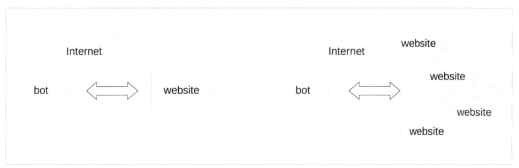

Figure 19.2, Standalone bot architectures.

A standalone bot architecture, also known as a non-distributed architecture, refers to an environment where the bot's operations and processing are hosted on a single piece of hardware. In contrast, a fully distributed bot architecture involves the use of multiple servers that are made to work together to handle the bot's operations.

When to consider a standalone architecture

While they have limitations, there are cases where a standalone bot environment is the right environment.

> You may want to use a standalone server on small projects, like the training exercises in this book, or feasibility studies. Even when the bot is scheduled to execute periodically, standalone architects should limit the number of times it accesses each source and limit the amount of data they store locally.

> Small standalone bots can be a good choice when your bot is running a one-time function. For example, if you need to parse all the references to names and

functions from a particular SEC Filing, you might only need to run that bot once. So many of the standard botOps guidelines are mitigated.

Another very valid reason to opt for the simpler standalone architecture is when your bot collects data from many sources—the more the better. Since you never want any of your bots to access any one server too often, it might be necessary to apply throttles or schedules that essentially make your bot less efficient. When your bot has the luxury of accessing many IP addresses, your bot can accomplish a lot of work during the periods that it would otherwise be give a source a rest.

Distributed systems

Most of the bot systems that I've been a part of have been *Distributed Systems*, or architectures that depend on multiple computers that share the workload in a networked environment. In such systems, servers take on specialized roles like: control and storage, graphics engines, password servers, etc.

Distributing tasks across multiple computer allows for a way to grow or extend a project to handle more users, more resources, or more functionality. Scaling also means ensuring it remains efficient and reliable as it grows in size and complexity.

A layer of control needs to be in place for a distributed bot architecture to work. For example, consider the managed distributed architecture suggested below in Figure 19.3.

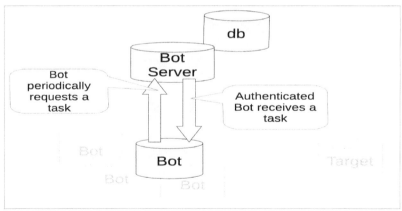

Figure 19.3, A managed, distributed, bot architecture

The bot server is essentially a web server, designed to accommodate the needs of bots that are either requesting a task to do, or bots that have data they need to put somewhere.

The bots are generally sleeping, but wake periodically to ask the bot server if there is a task to complete. My bots generally poll the central bot server every one or two minutes.

This initial communication serves the following purposes:

1. The bot authenticates itself to the bot server. This should be a fairly simple process as the bot's request shouldn't be totally unexpected. The bot server should expect the bot to be from a specific IP address or from a range of expected IP addresses. The bot should also present something to authenticate itself. This authentication might involve a simple password or certificate.

2. The bot may present some simple status information, indicating system memory available, or similar parameters.

3. But most importantly, the bot presents itself as available for the next task and waits for a response from the server.

Once the bot server identifies and authenticates the bot's request, it may look at the list of completed and uncompleted tasks in a task list in the database. If no tasks are available, the server will respond with a message, telling the bot to go back to sleep and ask for another opportunity at another time.

If, on the other hand, there is a task for the bot to complete, the bot server should supply the bot with everything it needs to complete the given task. This includes all URLs, passwords, and parsing information the bot needs. This might sound like a lot of code to send the bot, but most Selenium Python programs are only a few thousand bytes in size —or roughly the size of an online image. The bot simply saves the scripts received from the bot server to the file system, and executes them.

The amount of data sent to the bot will vary from project and task. In my projects, I tend to download multiple files. That way libraries can be kept separate from active code and raw data files. And while it may sound excessive to send ten files or 30k worth of instruction to a bot to perform on single tasks, it really doesn't task the system in any way.

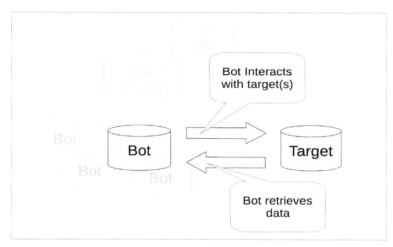

Figure 19.4, Bot interactions with the target website(s)

Any communication back to the central server, should also be programmed into the downloaded code. Once the bot complete's it's task, it should also delete the code used to perform the previous task.

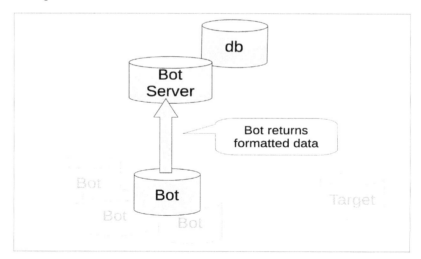

Figure 17.5, Uploading the data to the bot server

236

The central bot server accepts the new data (after authenticating the bot, of course) and puts it into the database. It will also mark that task as completed, credit the completion to that bot, and timestamp when the data was recorded.

Sometimes, and this shouldn't happen too often, the bot is unable to complete the task. When this happens, the central server will reassign the task to another bot after a period of time has elapsed. If that task can't be completed after the second or third attempt, that task will be shut down until someone can evaluate the situation.

Advantages of distributed systems

I have used variations of this theme for most of the 25 years I've been writing bots. And now that you have an idea of how such a system works, let's look at some potential advantages.

> It's very easy to scale a system like this. As long as the central server and sources can handle the load, you can literally double the system's capacity by doubling the number of bots.

> Distributed systems are more robust than non-distributed systems, though the central server remains a single point of failure. Otherwise, failure of any individual bot my impact performance, but it won't break the system.

> Systems—where a bot receives everything it needs to perform a task suffer from a little more overhead. But, that is mitigated by being much easier to update and maintain. I learned this the first time I had to individually update a set of twenty bots by hand every time there was a software update.

> The system described could gain a geographic advantage by strategically placing the bots on networks around the city or around the world. A distributed architecture can place bots closer to their sources or within specific monetary or time zones.

> When the instructions, download by the server to the bots are segregated into function specific files, the developer has an opportunity to library and simplify complex operations. Doing the same, without the access to known libraries or

data structures only adds to complexity and the urge to repeatedly "reinvent the wheel".

In summary, a non-distributed bot architecture might be sufficient for smaller-scale deployments with limited user interactions. As the bots capacity and complexity grows, the limitations of a non-distributed architecture can become more apparent. A fully distributed bot architecture may offer better scalability, reliability, and performance.

Bot architecture in 60 seconds

Scaling bots can be problematic because they often operate too efficiently, which can lead to aggressive behavior in terms of frequent access to target websites. This aggressive behavior can strain network bandwidth and chew-up excessive CPU cycles.

It's important to emphasize the need to be cautious when scaling bot operations to avoid overloading target websites. This chapter includes a cautionary tale involves collecting court records too quickly and receiving a warning message from a state court system.

All of the example bot demos in Section II use standalone bot architectures, where a bot is self-contained, stores data locally, and doesn't support remote control. These architectures are suitable for small projects or one-time functions, where there's no need for extensive scaling.

Distributed bot systems are configurations of multiple computers work together in a networked environment. The advantages of distributed systems include scalability, robustness, ease of maintenance, and geographic flexibility.

CHAPTER 20, FAULT TOLERANCE

Fault tolerance is important for all deployed software. But for bots, fault tolerance becomes a little more mission critical. This is because when a bot fails, it potentially jeopardizes the entire project because a bot's discovery can lead to the discovery of competitive intelligence campaigns, etc. The easiest way to ensure that your project is discovered is by developing a bot that looks more like a bot than a sentient person.

What is your current email address?

Sorry, I'm not sure how to answer that question.

What is your current email address?

Figure 20.1 Bots being bots

One way to ensure that your bot looks like a machine is to do things that people either wouldn't, or can't, do. We touched on a couple of those things earlier. This list includes things like:

Instantaneously filling in a text bots,

Not allowing time during a drag-and-drop operation,

Advancing to parsing a page before it could have possibly been read by a person,

Repeating a process too often,

Navigating to pages that don't exist, or

Essentially doing anything too quickly.

Earlier I touched on the fact that the worse kinds of logs to leave are ones which generate error conditions and leave records in error log files. And I as explained before, error logs are more apt to get attention form admins than simple access logs. And unfortunately sloppy bots are apt to leave error logs due to poor fault tolerance.

Fault tolerance becomes uniquely important to bots because, unlike other software, a bot's environment continually changes, as websites get updated. And when a page is no longer where you expect it to be you will generate a 404 error when you request that resource.

Another area where your bot can fail catastrophically is when a form that the bot uses changes. Here, a change as simple as renaming a form element can immediately cause a serious 500 series error and reveal that a bot is in use, for the simple reason that a person could not have generated that error by using a browser as expected.

Verify first

Never assume that a form variable, web page, or for that matter any other online resource will be available just because it was available when you developed the bot. Here are a few things to consider:

> When you want to go to the next page in your process, it is much better to follow a link than to go directly to that page. This is because the page may have moved since you developed the bot. And going to a nonexistent page is a sure way of announcing you are a bot.

> If you are following a link, verify that it is visible and otherwise available to a web user. Many times, Web Masters will insert invisible links into web pages to see who follows them. If these links exists, but aren't visible to people, those that follow those links are certainly bots.

> When you design a form submission, remember that you are designing from a snapshot of what that form looked like when you developed your code. So, before your bot submits a form, examine the page and make sure the method, action URL, and form variables have not changed. Again, if you submit a form that no longer exists,.or has been modified, you are be announcing that you are not human because a person would correctly use the form currently at the website.

Log, fail gracefully, and announce

When problems do arise, it's best that your bots are programmed to: log the issue, get out of the error condition gracefully, and announce that a problem has occurred.

As long as your bot is using the logging system from the framework defined in Section II, Project 2, a log is generated on just about every bot event. Not only is it useful to watch the console log the process of a bot during development, but it's especially useful to go back to the log files that are also created, to spot a problem with a bot that ran an hour ago, but has stopped running due to a problem.

Most of the time, a Selenium Python program will simply stop execution when it encounters an error. This is a very good thing. In earlier times, when I wrote bots with simpler technologies, the language would permit the bot to continue operating, even though an important communication with the target website had failed. In contrast, Selenium bots tend to *Fail Gracefully by nature*, and not create other problems when they encounter an error.

Additionally, it is always a good idea to communicate when a production server finds an error. This communication could be as simple as an auto generated email to the responsible developer.

Parsing and fault tolerance

We've mentioned the importance of of using landmarks, or text strings that you expect to find on specific web pages, before assuming that our bot ended up on the right web page. For example, let's say that we want to parse references to all the images on a web page. But before we do that, it's smart to verify that there is at least one image on the page. Otherwise, our `libBot.parseArray()` function will break because one of the important input parameters is missing. After one has suffered from a few of these failures, one learns the benefit of code like that in Script 20.1.

```
########################################################################
# Look for the existence of a landmark before using it as a landmark
if(libParse.stristr(html, '<img'))
    arrImgTags = libParse.parseArray(html, '<img', '>', INCL)
else
    libBot.writeLog(LOGPATH, "No Images were found in html")
```

Script 20.1, Checking the existence of a landmark before using it

A similar technique can be applied by using the Python try/except constructs, as shown in the following script.

```
########################################################################
# Testing the success of parseArray() and dealing with it's failure
try:
    arrImgTags = libParse.parseArray(html, '<img', '>', INCL)
except:
    libBot.writeLog(LOGPATH, "No Images were found in html")
```

Script 20.2 Using the Python exception handling

Selenium automatically handles many situations

It's important not to forget all the things that Selenium does automatically through the use of Webdriver. For example, all of the following error producing procedures are handled automatically by Selenium.

> Selenium performs all cookie management. This sounds like a small thing until you try to do if with code that you've written yourself. Cookie management involves writing and updating all the cookies that the server writes to the client on a user by user basis. Additionally, the browser automatically presents unexpired cookies back to the target web server in the request header. All things that we don't want to have to think about, or get wrong.

> When browsing, Selenium will automatically take any page forwarding directions provided either as part of an `HTTP Location:` or from a JavaScript command.

> Since we're operating in a browser, we get to piggyback on it's ability to handle SSL encryption layers.

In summary

The chapter emphasizes the importance of designing bots with fault tolerance in mind to ensure their reliability and avoid detection while operating in dynamic web environments. It also highlights how Selenium can help automate various aspects of fault-tolerant behavior, such as cookie management and page navigation.

Fault tolerance is critical for all software, but it's even more crucial for bots. Bot failures can jeopardize projects and may lead to the discovery of competitive intelligence campaigns.

To ensure that bots don't appear as machines, they shouldn't perform actions that humans typically wouldn't or couldn't do.

Bots operate in environments that frequently change. When web pages move or forms change, errors can occur. Bots should never assume that a resource will be available just because it was when the bot was developed. Verification before actions is crucial to avoid errors and detection.

Bots should be programmed to log issues, exit error conditions gracefully, and announce when a problem occurs.

Before parsing data from a web page, it's wise to verify the existence of landmarks or specific text strings.

Selenium and WebDriver provide automatic handling of various error-prone procedures. This includes cookie management, page forwarding, and SSL encryption, which Selenium manages internally, simplifying these tasks for bot developers.

CHAPTER *21, MACHINES AS HUMANS*

After more than twenty-five years of bot development experience, the one thing that stuck with me is the importance of making your bots look as human as possible. Because unlike other types of software, bots have the potential to create true competitive advantages for the people that run them. As such, organizations that view bots as part of their digital infrastructure really don't want to "show their hand" to their competitors and revel a trade secret.

Bots are a trade secret

If you exclusively use your bots to test your own, or a client's, web pages, then you obviously don't care if people know that your deploying bots, because those people are probably paying you to do so. And, at this point, everyone uses bots to test and maintain their websites. But, if your bot is creating some type of competitive advantage—for example collecting market data from your competitors, you should protect that secret.

Competitive Intelligence is often confused with *Business Intelligence.* The difference between Business Intelligence and Competitive Intelligence is that Business Intelligences focus on what's happening *inside* your business, while Competitive Intelligence is fixated on what happens *outside* your business, This chapter deals mostly with bots used in Competitive Intelligence campaigns, or those activities that give your organization a better idea of what's happening *outside* your organization.

Some of the trade secrets your bots may generate may include:

What your competitors charge for products and services,

Who your competitors are looking to hire,

What percentage of your market do you control?

How big is your market?

Who's healthier? Your business or your market at large?

What changes are your competitors making?

What are your competitors' retail strategies?

How can I be the first to know or act when an event occurs?

The list of intelligence that can be collected and analyzed during a Competitive Intelligence campaign can be varied and unique. But the thing they all have in common is that they are trade secrets; and as such, they need protection. So, your strategies also need protection. And if your strategy includes bots, you need to lower your profile by making your bots look less like bots.

Stealthy ≠ sketchy

As soon as the topic of *stealthy bots,* or bots that are hard to detect, comes into a conversation, people often assume some sketchy activity is going on. This is largely due to people not understanding how bots are used and what their value is to an organization. Once management understands that their bots are delivering value to the organization, their attitude shifts. Suddenly, their bots are a top trade secret that they only discuss in closed-door meetings with the right people. As such, developers need to also honor the need to keep one's company secrets secret. And if you develop bots, that means writing *stealthy bots*, or bots that are hard to detect because they are indistinguishable from people using the same resource.

> The goal isn't to develop bots that avoid all detection, but to build bots that don't disclose trade secrets. Your next goal should be to operate your bot as though it is a reasonable human.

How bots get discovered

The danger in not running bots as though they were humans is—because like human visitors, bots leave records of their activity in the server logs of the websites they visit. These logs create a permanent record of every web page, image, or scrap of JavaScript you've ever requested from the server. These records are archived in a timestamped log, along with—at a minimum, your IP address, and potentially the ISP of your domain, any information the server previously stored in cookies, and other identifying information.

This is important to at least consider, because the domain recorded in your access logs could be your employer's public domain name, if your bots run onsite. So just as you browse with some degree of discretion, you should also ask for the same discretion from your bots.

My experience is that few server admins look at server logs, unless there are issues. This is in one regard a good thing, because if you make a careless mistake with your bot and needlessly reveal a uniquely identifying information, you probably won't see any consequences. But on the other hand, if you're bot causes errors you will also create records in a server error log, which is much more apt to receive attention. So you specifically want your bot to avoid committing 400 and 500 series HTTP errors.

Having run IT departments in the past, I know that resources are often limited and admins simply don't have the luxury of time to gaze over server logs. So many IT departments are apt to apply security software to automatically monitor their logs for mischief. If questionable activity is discovered a threshold, known as a "*tripwire*" is crossed and someone gets notified, usually immediately via a text message.

Reasons NOT to fear discovery of your bot

Before we explore why you may not want your bot to be discovered, lets talk about the bad reasons to design your bots to avoid discovery.

Don't be stealthy to break a law

You should not design a stealthy, human-traited, bot to violate any laws, whether they relate to privacy, security, or other matters. These are particularly dangerous crimes because writing a bot to deliberately commit a crime shows intent. So, it's a stupid crime to commit and not likely something a developer would do unintentionally.

Furthermore, there's plenty of legitimate work for bot writers in the areas of:

- Data Warehousing,

- Data Journalism,

- Test Engineering,

- Competitive Intelligence,

- Political Action,

- Law Enforcement,

- Auditing, and

- Just about any other sector.

But all of the bots running in any of the areas above will run more effectively if they look like people when they run.

When your bot needs to authenticate itself

In many cases, I've been asked to develop bots that access web pages with restricted access. In those cases, the bot needs to use a password, a digital signature key, and sometimes *Two Factor Authentication* (or a secondary form of communication to prove one's identity) to access these web pages. Additionally, you may have to surrender personally identifying information to obtain credentials to access a website. If you're working in any area that resembles finance, it is not uncommon to have to surrender your Social Security Number, as well as a corporate email address. Obviously, when your bot logs into a website, using credentials like these, the target website knows you're there. And at some early point, you need to decide—for competitive, contractual, or what-have-you reasons, how important it is to conceal your using a bot.

You usually cannot conceal your bot's identity when it accesses information behind a paywall, or other protected areas. But that shouldn't be a big concern because the goal, again, isn't to be anonymous, the goal is to not look like a bot. In these cases, where a bot uses private data, consider that your bot is a proxy for the person, whose credentials where given at login. And by "be a proxy", your bot should operate a humanly sustainable pace. Things like repetition are easier to resolve or are at least more plausible than an inhuman rate of operation.

Stealthiness falls into two areas

There are generally two families of design factors that can help ensure that your bots remain stealthy and undiscovered. We'll look into the first, adopting human traits, first and then discuss the need for extra fault tolerance.

Looking human

One area involves designing paths for your bot that look and appear to be legitimately human in the server logs. While these traits will be explored in detail later, for now assume these traits reflect basic human activity. For example, people will not download a web page every day at the exact same time for months. Another example is that people need some time to evaluate the contents on a web page before they move on. In contrast, allowing your bot to execute lines of Selenium Python code as quickly as possible is a sure-fire way to set-off one of the before mentioned security tripwires.

Fault tolerance

The other aspect of stealthy botOps more closely falls into the category of fault tolerance. While fault tolerance is important in every field of software development, it's probably more critical when you need to act stealthy and the faults are different and less obvious.

The fourteen rules to writing stealthy bots

Now that you know the legitimate reasons for writing stealthy bots, there are a number of things you can do to make you bots—not disappear, but look more human.

Rule number one: Be kind

The number one rule—above all other rules, is to be kind to each and every one of the websites your bots visit. If for no other reason, you don't want to invest time and energy into a useful piece of software, hopefully one that provides a valuable competitive advantage, and then have one of your target websites block you because you are exhibiting some type of competitive advantage. Or worse, you don't want to reveal a competitive trade secret to anyone. And bots are often a strategic part of that strategic equation.

Don't go too fast

The first time you see a Selenium Python bot running at full speed you may think that you've found that greatest efficiency machine made to mankind. This is because Selenium Python can be programmed to use web resources at ridiculously high speeds. These speeds look ridiculous because they are so much faster than what we've seen people do with browsers. Which is precisely why you want to slow your bots down!

If you want your bot to look human, it should run at human-like speeds. The result of not doing this is to potentially download pages so fast that you create a condition that looks like a *DOS or DDOS* (Denial of Service, or Distributed Denial of Service) attack. And while I'm sure that most of you would never want to do this, it's extremely easy to do in development if care isn't applied.

 For a retail client, I once built a series of bots that analyzed competing stores to determine various market factors. At the time, the work was spread across ten bots. Each bot had a refresh cycle of one minute and returned anywhere from one to forty product descriptions per cycle. So collectively, the bots fed anywhere from ten to four hundred product descriptions to a central server per minute. This didn't seem like extensive loading, and the server responded just fine. However, the hosting company saw unusual traffic going to my server and concluded that my server was under attack. I was unable to explain to them what I was doing and had to use a different host (AWS).

Embrace randomness

People are never predictable, so your your bots should also be unpredictable. Here are a couple of commonly overlooked ways to inject unpredictability in your bot designs.

> If your bot is running on an automated schedule, don't always launch your bot at the same time. I also like to run a slightly different schedule every day. Additionally, my bots seldom work on weekends or holidays and I will frequently schedule coffee and lunch breaks into their automated schedules.

Insert random delays after each human step your bot takes. The `libBot.RandomWait()` function is a good one to use for this purpose, plus it logs when the pause happened, and the length of the duration.

When practical, it's a good practice to not always follow the same route while navigating a website. On simple websites, this trick may not always be feasible, but on larger websites, taking an occasional detour is recommended. For instance, it could be beneficial to permit your bot to click on a random link and sporadically return to the initial page, occurring randomly around 2% or 3% of the time. This approach will assist in emulating a human level of curiosity or error, which serves your goal of appearing more human-like in either scenario.

Don't look like your developing a bot

There are some botDev activities, or bad habits, that really need to be addressed if you want to produce a stealthy bot. For example, if you need to parse a page of text, don't repeatedly download that page every time you want to operate your parser while debugging during development. This may not seem like a big deal, but if you are unaware of how many times you request a live file from a target server, you may be surprised to learn that you've download that same file 40, 80, 120 times during the course of your bot's development, validation, or test phases. It's a much better practice to download the file you need for development and save it to a file. Then access the local file instead repeatedly requesting the identical file from the target server.

Use normal sized browser windows

As a developer, you may be tempted to run bots in unusually large or small browser windows. For instance, a developer may find that running bots in a 10x10 pixel window is an advantage because, with this technique, you can run a number of bots simultaneously, without much screen clutter. If you do this, be aware that modern browsers send a fair amount of user environmental information, made available in the `Window.Navigator` object (discussed in Chapter 15). These parameters are passed back to the server so developers can better gauge their audience and better calibrate the user experience they deliver[21]. So parameters like screen size, operating system, etc. are widely used to adapt application for both mobile and desktop use. But repeatedly using browser windows of ridiculous sizes may be incriminating.

Run your bots when the server is busiest

This point may sound counter intuitive. If rule number one is to be kind to our sources, wouldn't we want to run our bots when the server is least busy? Probably not; here's why.

> When you run your bot during max use times, your access log entries get merged with everyone else's. And if you want to make a point of not allowing your bot from standing out from the crowd, you want your log entries to be as inconspicuous as possible. So when it's an option, mix your server log records with as many other records as possible.

> It may not always be optimal to run your bots during peak usage times. But if you need to run your bots off-hours, consider that many websites go down for unannounced maintenance at unscheduled periods in the wee hours of the day.

> Another thing that can happen during a servers "off-hours" is that the administrator may have scheduled either web server or database server back-ups. These activities are frequently left to periods of low activity because they can adversely affect server performance. If you're bot needs to run during these periods, ensure that it can accommodate poor server response.

If you're not sure when a server's peak service times are, you can ping the server at various times to establish what average response times are. You may be tempted to write a comprehensive bot to record a server's access times over a week, or so. But if you do something like this, know that your bot will look a lot like a *reConBot*, (or a reconnaissance bot)—which it is, if other precautions on are used.

Follow links instead of going to URLs

When your bot needs to go to the next web page, it's always best to get there via a link from one of the variations of the `driver.find_element(By.LINK)` commands

---

21 If you are familiar with PHP, these environmental parameters are passed in the $_SERVER array.

252

instead of using a `driver.go(URL)` command. The simple reason for this is that the link that once pointed to the URL you plan to send your bot to may have changed. And, if you go to that URL after then link changed, you're going to look like you're using automation to get to that page. It's much safer to first validate that the link is still on the page, and then click on the link than it is to assume that the web page your requesting is for an existing page. This may sound like a small thing, and you might rationalize that you can use Python's exception handling commands to manage missing pages, but you are still leaving records in log files. And if the page isn't there, the server will issue a HTTP 401 (page not found) error, which will appear in the more visible error log. This is something you don't want to have happen. And if your bot is automated, it's definitely not something your want to do hundreds of times in a day, which can happen if things are allowed to run awry.

Don't get lazy on form submission

When you're confronted with a web page that has a form using the GET method, don't use simply decode at submit the query string to access the next page. First, you don't know if the form's ACTION may have changed. And secondly, form elements may have been added or removed. A much better tactic is to rely on landmarks (from Chapter 18), and to submit the actual form.

Don't follow traps.

I can't mention the importance of following links without mentioning a bot killing technique that is sometimes employed by administrators, who want to identify bots on their website. The technique works like this. A link is provided on the a web page that goes to a special page that identifies the IP address of the user. This IP address is then placed on a black list of IP address that have lost access to the website. The administrator knows that a bot followed the link because the link was designed to not be visible to humans. This type of link—that is valid, but not visible, can be constructed in many ways, ranging from: making the link on a 0 pixel by 0 pixel image, or by placing some other web element over the top of the link. If you are writing anything that looks like a spider, that follows links. You may want to find a way to validate the links before they are used.

Rotate IP addresses

There are few things more embarrassing than spending a ton of money to build-out a system of bots that do something cool and useful, like evaluating pricing on your competitors website, only to find that your competitor found your IP address in their logs, and traced it back to your corporate servers. The result of such a finding could lead to retaliation of some type, and certainly the loss of a resource.

The scenario above is the reason you never want to host a competitive bot on your own, identifiable, network. The solution is to use an IP address that can't be traced back to you. Or, you may want to go through a service that provides proxies that rotate their outgoing gateway to continually change their IP address. This is because it is much easier to point your browser's proxy address at their server than it is to rotate, and maintain a network, IP addresses on your own. These services can be found with a Google search and are capable of switching IP address ever few seconds from a pool of hundreds of IP addresses for a very nominal price. Believe me, it's best to contract this out.

I would caution against is using any of the free proxy servers available online. First, these servers tend to get a lot of traffic, and are not always reliable. Secondly, many if not most of these free proxy servers are actually poorly configured Microsoft Exchange Servers, and are acting as a proxy unintentionally. Additionally, there is absolutely nothing to keep the owners of these free proxies to monitor traffic and it is rumored that many of these servers are run by governments. If you want privacy, use a reputable VPN (Virtual Private Network) provider.

Delete cookies

It may be advantageous to strategically delete your cookies. This is especially true if you are cycling your IP addresses, or if you use the header rotation suggested next. This is because if any identifying information is written as a cookie, that information will again be accessible by the server if you're using a proxy—thereby blowing your cover. I suggest deleting your cookies every time you fire-up your bot.

Rotate HTTP request headers

If you want your bots to surf anonymously, you might want to make your browser selection look like everyone else. That's why I will occasionally create an array of browser User Agent Names and randomly select one to use before a session. This is done in the routine in `lib.Selenium` that configures Webdriver. I highly suggest that you only try to spoof modern browsers as the browser selected may influence website performance and features.

Distribute tasks among multiple bots

If there is a lot of work for your bot to accomplish, you may want to explore one of the distributed architectures that are described in Chapter 19, on Scaling and architectures. These techniques are worth visiting if you need to scale your bot without looking like you're scaling a bot.

Honor your referrer variable

When you click on a link, one of the pieces of metadata your browser sends to the server is the referring URL, or the page where you took the link. This `REFERRER` is useful for many instances ranging from gauging the effectiveness of SEO campaigns to enforcing security. This isn't something you need to worry about with Selenium, because this is done automatically when you click on a link. But if you are using cURL, or some other method to access files, you might want to make sure your `REFERRER` value makes sense.

I once very nearly made the following mistake. I had developed a bot for a client that used a proprietary dashboard to show the results of what that bots discovered. The mistake I made was I put links to a vendor website on the dashboard. The result was that the URL of that page on the dashboard was transmitted to the vendor in the REFERRER variable. Since we wanted the dashboard, and the project, to remain a secret, I had to write some additional code to strip away the referrer to avoid tipping my client's hand, and at least partially revealing the strategy we were employing with bots.

In summary

The chapter emphasizes the importance of creating bots that appear as human as possible, particularly in the context of Competitive Intelligence campaigns. The value of concealing bot activities to protect trade secrets and competitive strategies.

Key points include:

Competitive Intelligence focuses on external factors affecting a business, such as competitor activities, market trends, and pricing strategies. It contrasts with Business Intelligence, which looks inward at a company's internal data and processes. In Competitive Intelligence, it's crucial to use stealthy bots that mimic human behavior to avoid detection. These bots are designed to collect data discreetly, protecting the organization's strategies and insights.

Bots leave traces in server logs, including IP addresses and access patterns. While few server administrators regularly review logs, automated security software may detect suspicious activity and trigger notifications.

Ethical considerations are highlighted, emphasizing that stealthy bots should not be used to violate laws or harm others. Legitimate use cases for bots are discussed, ranging from data warehousing to competitive intelligence.

The chapter offered practical tips for designing stealthy bots, including:

- Running bots at human-like speeds.

- Introducing randomness in bot behavior.

- Varying access times to avoid patterns.

- Following links instead of directly accessing URLs.

- Handling form submissions properly.

- Avoiding traps set by administrators to detect bots.

- Rotating IP addresses and using proxy services.

- Deleting cookies and rotating HTTP request headers.

- Distributing tasks among multiple bots, and

- Ensuring the "Referrer" metadata is coherent with browsing behavior.

Running bots during peak usage times can help blend in with other user activities, making them less conspicuous in server logs.

Don't use free proxy servers due to potential unreliability and security concerns, suggesting the use of reputable VPN providers instead.

CHAPTER 22, BIG DATA, BIG HEADACHE

Big data might be useful and important, but I'll tell you… if you ever need to move it, big data becomes a real liability. This chapter aims to provide some easy, reusable, steps to making the transfer of data less awful.

According to the US Chamber of Commerce, it's estimated that over 90% of the world's data was generated in just the past two years. Much of this data is generated by bots. The problem is that the data is seldom consumed where it is sourced. So that means that the data needs to be moved from the bots to some type of database, as discussing in the topic of Bot Architectures in Chapter 19.

It turns out the process of transferring data from one location to another is more significant and complex than what most people would perceive. This chapter examines the issues involved with moving data, and provides a series of time worn tips to simplify the process.

Big data is hard to move

There are a number of issues involved with moving data from one place to another. Most of these concerns are related to the potential scale of the data moved.

Data transfer projects should consider all of the following.

Infrastructure

Large data sets require massive storage capacity. This applies to the related test data, back-ups, as well as to production data. So, that 12 terabyte database can quickly become a 24 or 36 terabyte database.

Datasets of this size aren't just theoretical, they're physical and they take-up actual space on storage devices, consume power, and create heat. Additionally, there are few opportunities to put that much data on a single storage device. So your data architect will need to figure out how to segment the data either functionally, or by physically partitioning the data across multiple storage devices.

Transfer speeds

Data is typically transferred serially, one bit at a time. If one assumes two more bits for overhead and a 150 Mbps transfer rate, it would take roughly a minute to transfer one gigabyte of data.

In the example above, it will take just over a minute (66.67 seconds) to transfer 1 gigabyte of data over a 150 megabit channel. It will, however, take a bit longer than that because something on the other end will consume time while processing that data. So there will be additional delays caused by communication with storage devices and internal networks. Additionally, consuming data at this rate also means that the receiving server won't have many additional resources available for doing anything else. All of these delays, of course, jeopardize live or real time data access.

Data security

Any time data is moved it is exposed to both data breaches and data loss. Robust systems can detect data integrity issues and request that the broken data be retransmitted. But of course, this also consumes even more time. In fact, just having the capability to detect incomplete data will consume time, whether data needs to be retransmitted or not.

Data heterogeneity

Data, from separate sources, needs to be identified the same way and have the same type casting. For example, whatever comprises an Order Number from one source also needs to be referenced and identified as an Order Number when it comes from another source.

Data, however, may be sourced from multiple places. Additionally, often only part of the data is sourced at one place, and other related data comes from somewhere else. This can cause redundancy in data field names and other problems. Sometimes, for the same of conformity, sourced data needs to be split, parsed or combined to meet the requirements of a database.

Resource management

As read in Chapter 19, on bot architecture, data can be sourced by many parallel machines, all reporting back to a single server. When one bot sends data to a server it will take a finite amount of resources (memory, CPU cycles, and time) to:

> Verify the contents of the data,
>
> Identify if the data requires a new database record, or an update of an existing one, and
>
> Writing the data. One bot sending data to a centralized server is very manageable, but fifty bots that present data every minute, can be another story. A barrage of data from bots can sometimes resemble a self-inflicted Denial of Service Attack.

All of these things take time and add to the burden of quickly moving around large amounts of data.

Cost

The final consideration is cost. Everything that big data touches (memory, bandwidth, CPU time) costs money. And the bigger the data, the more things it touches, the more the cost goes up. And as mentioned earlier, all of this storage has physical volume, power consumption, maintenance, cooling issues, and other related physical properties and needs that the end user seldom considers.

Data transfer goals: reusable and fool-proof

If we're going to put our attention to developing some proprietary process, the area of data transport would be a good place to start. There are, in fact, a number of things that can be done to make data transfer a plug-and-play activity.

Here are some worthy goals for a data transport process.

> The system needs to be reusable. In other words, the code that does the data transfer should be a well debugged project that works in various applications with little to no modification.

> The system needs a fool-proof way to match collected records with those in the database. This might mean the creation of a "universal API" that can process and store various formats of data.

The value of CSV files

One of the best decisions I made was to require, in my projects, that bots collect and store data in local *CSV*, or Comma Separated Value files as we did in Section II Project 6. There were other formats to consider, including: SQL statements, JSON, and XML. Any of these would work, but I chose to use CSV because they: have low overhead, are easy to create without using special software, are easily read (and their format verified) by any spread sheet software.

Additionally, it's easy to build a CSV file over time, and upload it to a server when needed. This sequence of building CSV files, uploading them, deleting the old CSV file and starting over, is also resource friendly to the receiving server. So far, I haven't triggered any tripwires.

The quest for a universal API

It seemed that I had to write a new interface every time I need a bot to upload data to a server. This was because data formats weren't formalized, and rules for importing data seemed to change from application to application. These interfaces can become a real time sink when many interfaces need to be written. I needed to find a more universal way to upload data to a server and have it imported once it got there.

I already decided to adopt CSV files as the data file standard. The next step in that regard was to find a universal way to upload a CSV file. One can use any number of methods to move a file from one pace to another. Since my bot is already using Selenium, a web interface to the database seems natural. As long as you are connected to a web server using the https protocol, you should be fine.

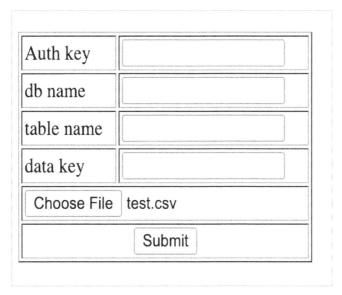

Figure 22.1, Uploading data to a server using an HTML form.

The other security steps I like to include is some type of Authentication key. If it's not in a Cookie or the HTTP Header, this isn't a bad place to put it. Additionally, it's a good idea to check the IP address and verify that it belongs to an agent you control.

By defining the database and table names, the developer can direct this data to any number of destinations.

Each record in the database should have a *unique identifier* or a key. Sometimes this is easy. For example, if you're recording records of cars, the VIN, or Vehicle Identification Number can be used to uniquely identify any vehicle. Likewise, Employee Numbers, Licenses, EINs, ISBNs, Phone Numbers, email addresses, UPC, or any standard identification system can be used. Sometimes, this unique identifier might be a combination of data cells (like name, address, city, state, and postal code). Regardless of what your data uses to uniquely identify records, it should be communicated to the receiving server. Without a unique identifier, there is no way for the receiving software to know if the record is new, and should be inserted, or if the data us already in the database and needs to be updated.

Since we have Selenium in our pocket, we can initiate a file upload with a line of script as shown in Script 22.1, assuming you have a server with the Universal API on the other end.

```
driver.get("_SERVER_?fileName=CSVfile.csv&db=yourDB&table=dbTable&key=PHONE&Auth=123!@#
```
Script 22.1, Initiating data importation with a simple REST request

The GET method shown in Script 22.1 tells the host server a number of important things. Let's look at the passed parameters in the order they appear.

> **CSVfile.csv** is the name of the CSV file you previously loaded to the server. You may want to pass the entire path to the file, or leave it as a relative reference.

> **db** is the name of the database you want the host server to use as a final destination for the data in the CSV file.

> **table** is the name of the data table in the previously defined database. This table has column names that match the column names in the CSV file.

> **key** is the name of the CSV file column that holds each records unique identifier, or *key*. In this case, it was decided to use people's phone numbers as

264

the key identifier. In other cases a different identifier may be used, for example: email addresses, Customer IDs, Drivers License Numbers. These keys are primarily used to by the universal API to decide if the received data is new data, or data tif hat should update an existing record.

Sometimes—but not in cases covered in this book, there are other reasons to use multiple keys. For example, one might combine the DATE and PHONE columns to track changes and trends.

Association between CSV file and database table

For this to work well, in multiple situations, a little planning must take place. Actually, not that much planning at all. Once you design your database table, with column names, indexes, and relationships as your schema requires, the next step is to ensure that when your bot transmits a CSV file to the universal API, that the columns in the CSV file directly match columns in the database table.

It's important to point out that the CSV does not have to have ALL of the columns in the entire database table, but the columns must match for the ones it has, and that one of those columns is a unique identifier, or key, for that row of data.

The image in Figure 22.2 does a good job of showing this relationship.

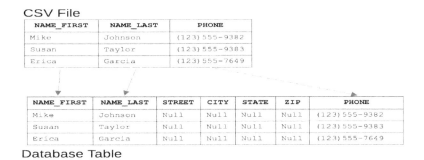

Figure, 22.2 Relation ship between CSV file and database table where PHONE is the key

265

Once the host server receives the file and is notified that the file is ready for importation, all that has to happen is:

```
The server authenticates the incoming data and it's source.

The server iterates over each row of data, and for each row:

        Inserts a new record into the database, if the phone number
        is new, or

        Updates an existing database record with the matching phone
        number.
```

Obviously, the pseudocode above could be made more robust and production ready. Filters and other processes could be added. But the simple process of implementing a universal API—used over and over again, has saved me countless hours. Who knows, maybe it saved me enough time to write a book.

The beauty of this system is that bots can upload incomplete data and still have it processed and imported into the database. You can even use separate keys on different passes if more than one uniquely identifiable piece of data exists.

A big data summary

Some of the pains in managing large amounts of data include:

> Scale and Infrastructure, Transfer Speeds, Data Security, Data Heterogeneity, Resource Management and Cost Considerations.

Storing data in CSV format is a resource-friendly approach.

> Upload data to a server with methods like HTML form uploads and secure authentication protocols.

> Initiate data importation with a REST request providing essential information like file name, database, table, and key identifier.

> Maintain consistency between CSV file columns and database table columns is vital for smooth data importation.

> A key identifier, such as a phone number, links the CSV file to the database table.

The universal API, used repeatedly, saves time and effort in data importation. It accommodates incomplete data uploads and supports multiple unique identifiers for data matching and importation.

CHAPTER 23, CHROME INSPECT

Google Chrome's Inspect[22] is a powerful set of tools that allow developers to inspect, debug, and analyze web pages and web applications. This tools spares the developer of many hours of searching through source code and hoping that they've accurately identified the web objects Selenium need to interact with.

Chrome Inspect is a fairly large tool set, with a total of eleven features that are broadly useful to web developers. In fact, Chrome Inspect has one of the better JavaScript debuggers.

We will mention each of these other Inspect features so you can explore them based on your own need. But as bot developers, there are two features that make Chrome Inspect worth learning.

Chrome Inspect is by far, the easiest way to:

1. Inspect and identify web elements, and calculate their XPATH.
2. Directly read and write cookies.

Identifying web objects

The most important function, for our purposes is the ability to select and examine individual HTML elements on a web page. It provides a detailed view of the HTML structure, CSS styles, and associated properties of the selected element. It also allows calculation of XPATHs and other useful data.

As we've learned, identifying web objects is one of the fundamental parts of using Selenium, because Selenium can only manipulate or read web objects that you can identify. Here's how to identify web objects using Chrome Inspect.

---

22   Chrome Inspect is also known as Developer Tools or DevTools.

Let's suppose that we want to identify the web objects that is the search button in Figure 23.1 below. To identify this button—and at this point we're only assuming it's a button, simply cursor your mouse over the item and right mouse click, as shown below in Figure 23.1.

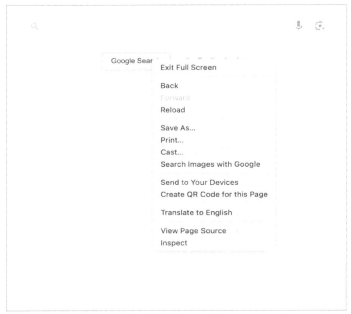

Figure 23.1, Invoking Chrome Inspect to identify an object on a web page.

Once this small window appears, slide your mouse down to Inspect and left click the mouse. What happens next is the magic shown in Figure 23.2.

Figure 23.2, Chrome Inspect identifying a web object.

The highlighted section in Figure 23.2 is a detail of the HTML, and often JavaScript, that defines the web object responsible for the search submit button. Of the data in the highlighted area, the most important to a bot developer are shown in Figure 23.3.

#	Parameter	Value
	Class	"gNO89b"
	Value	"Google Search"
	Name	"btnK"
	Id	Not used
	Type	Submit
	XPATH	/html/body/div[1]/div[3]/form/div[1]/div[1]/div[4]/center/input[1]

Figure 23.3, Parameters of interest from highlighted area

As you should already know, we could write a line of Selenium Python to click on the button of interest with the following line of code shown in Script 23.1.

```
```
Two methods of identifying the same submit button
```

# clicking on an object, identified by NAME
driver.find_element(By.NAME, "btnK").click()

# clicking on an object, identified by XPATH
xpath = "/html/body/div[1]/div[3]/form/div[1]/div[1]/div[4]/center/input[1]";
driver.find_element(By.XPATH, xpath).click()
```

Script 23.1, Using name and xpath to locate a submit button

While in this case the NAME parameter was available to use, but it isn't the only identifier we could have used. Often the item's ID is available. And when either the ID or NAME are available, they should get preference over others[23]. When no usable identifier is available, the XPATH can always be used. Obtaining the XPATH requires one more step. To access the XPATH, and more parameters, right mouse over the highlighted area, click on Copy, and select the parameter you want to copy; in this case XPATH, as shown in the next Figure.

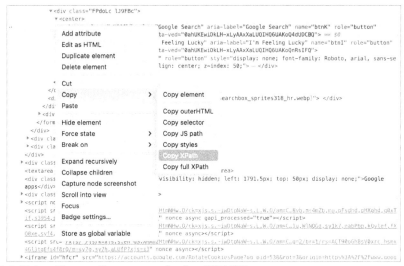

Figure 23.4, Using Chrome Inspect to calculate XPATHs

---

23 There is no logical reason to choose one locator over another, but if given the choice between NAME and ID, I'd likely select ID.

Manipulating cookies

Another key feature that Chrome Inspect delivers to bot developers is the ability to read and write *Cookies*. Cookies, as you know, are small pieces of data that websites write to browsers to maintain state in a stateless environment like the web. While cookies have many purposes, for the bot developer, they are mostly used in authentication and setting sessions, or to verify that sessions have ended.

You can access cookies in Chrome Inspect by clicking on Inspect's memory tab and select the cookies from the domain you want to view. It's that simple.

Other Chrome Inspect features

From a bot developer's standpoint, the ability to identify web objects, and to a lesser extent, to manipulate cookies, are the two most important features of Chrome Inspect. There are, however, more Inspect functions that you might find useful at some point in your development career. Here is a quick list of those other features.

> The Console tab provides an interactive JavaScript console that allows developers to execute JavaScript code directly within the context of the page. It's helpful for debugging and testing code snippets.

> The Network tab provides a detailed view of all the network requests made by the web page. It shows information about the request and response headers, status codes, load times, and resources used.

> The Sources tab allows developers to set breakpoints and debug JavaScript code directly within the browser. It provides a powerful debugging environment to step through code, inspect variables, and analyze call stacks.

> The Performance tab helps analyze and optimize the performance of a web page. It provides a timeline view of loading and rendering events, allowing developers to identify performance bottlenecks.

> In addition to facilitating cookie manipulation, the Memory tab assists in analyzing memory usage and identifying memory leaks in web applications. It provides insights into the memory consumption of different components on the page.

The Application tab provides access to various application storage mechanisms, such as Local Storage, Session Storage, IndexedDB, and Cookies. Developers can view and modify data stored in these storage types.

Inspect offers a mobile device emulation feature, enabling developers to test how web pages render and behave on different devices and screen sizes.

The Audits tab performs a set of automated tests on the web page to evaluate performance, accessibility, and other best practices. It provides suggestions for improving the page's overall quality.

The Security tab displays information about the page's security, including insecure content warnings and certificate details.

Accessibility Analysis: The Accessibility tab helps identify accessibility issues on the web page and offers suggestions to improve the accessibility of the content for users with disabilities.

In summary

Overall, Google Chrome Inspect is an essential tool for bot developers by providing tools to identify web objects and to manipulate cookies. It provides a comprehensive set of features for web page inspection, debugging, and performance optimization for web developers.

Section IV: Libraries

Here are complete listings for the libraries used in Section II. These scripts are also available for download at mepso.com. Scripts for the ten example bots are available at the end of each chapter in Section II. You should feel free to use these libraries for your own purposes. Just know that the responsibility of these libraries lays in the hands of the developer that uses them. (No one is making you use any of this code.) Each of these scripts were placed into the Public Domain through the W3C Software Notice and License. This section contains the following libraries:

- libPaths   Path definitions used by the Framework

- libBot   Various bot related functions

- libSelenium   Functions that load and control Webdriver

- libParse   Text parsing functions

W3C SOFTWARE NOTICE AND LICENSE

4.0 LIBPATHS.PY

```
################################################################################
#
# libPaths.py
#
# From the book: Developing Bots with Selenium Python, @2023 Michael Schrenk
# Usage via the W3C Software Notice and License (below).
#
################################################################################
# W3C SOFTWARE NOTICE AND LICENSE
# http://www.w3.org/Consortium/Legal/2002/copyright-software-20021231
#
# This work (and included software, documentation such as READMEs, or other
# related items) is being provided by the copyright holders under the following license.
# By obtaining, using and/or copying this work, you (the licensee) agree that you have
# read, understood, and will comply with the following terms and conditions.
#
# Permission to copy, modify, and distribute this software and its documentation, with or
# without modification, for any purpose and without fee or royalty is hereby granted,
# provided that you include the following on ALL copies of the software and documentation
# or portions thereof, including modifications:
#
#    1. The full text of this NOTICE in a location viewable to users of the redistributed
#       or derivative work.
#    2. Any pre-existing intellectual property disclaimers, notices, or terms and
#       conditions. If none exist, the W3C Software Short Notice should be included
#       (hypertext is preferred, text is permitted) within the body of any redistributed
#       or derivative code.
#    3. Notice of any changes or modifications to the files, including the date changes
#       were made. (We recommend you provide URIs to the location from which the code is
#       derived.)
#
# THIS SOFTWARE AND DOCUMENTATION IS PROVIDED "AS IS," AND COPYRIGHT HOLDERS MAKE NO
# REPRESENTATIONS OR WARRANTIES, EXPRESS OR IMPLIED, INCLUDING BUT NOT LIMITED TO,
# WARRANTIES OF MERCHANTABILITY OR FITNESS FOR ANY PARTICULAR PURPOSE OR THAT THE USE
# OF THE SOFTWARE OR DOCUMENTATION WILL NOT INFRINGE ANY THIRD PARTY PATENTS,
# COPYRIGHTS, TRADEMARKS OR OTHER RIGHTS.
#
# COPYRIGHT HOLDERS WILL NOT BE LIABLE FOR ANY DIRECT, INDIRECT, SPECIAL OR
# CONSEQUENTIAL DAMAGES ARISING OUT OF ANY USE OF THE SOFTWARE OR DOCUMENTATION.
#
# The name and trademarks of copyright holders may NOT be used in advertising or
# publicity pertaining to the software without specific, written prior permission.
# Title to copyright in this software and any associated documentation will at all
# times remain with copyright holders.
################################################################################

import sys
from datetime import datetime

# Pick Your environment
```

```
MAC = False
PC = True

# The log file is where the bot's logs are kept
timeStart = datetime.today().strftime('%Y%m%d_%H%M%S')
logFile                          = "LOG_" + timeStart + ".log"

# Determine the root path to the project
if MAC:
        pathRoot                         = "/YOUR_MAC_PROJECT_DIRECTORY"
if PC:
        pathRoot                         = "/YOUR_PC_PROJECT_DIRECTORY"
else:
        print("pathRoot cannot be determined.")
        sys.exit()

# Define where your libraries and Chromedriver live
pathLibs                         = pathRoot + "libs/"

# This is the location of the webdriver (Chromedriver)
pathChromeDriver         = pathLibs + "webdrivers/chromedriver"
```

278

4.1 libBot.py

```
###############################################################################
#
# libBot.py
#
# From the book: Developing Bots with Selenium Python, @2023 Michael Schrenk
# Usage via the W3C Software Notice and License (below).
#
###############################################################################
# W3C SOFTWARE NOTICE AND LICENSE
# http://www.w3.org/Consortium/Legal/2002/copyright-software-20021231
#
# This work (and included software, documentation such as READMEs, or other
# related items) is being provided by the copyright holders under the following license.
# By obtaining, using and/or copying this work, you (the licensee) agree that you have
# read, understood, and will comply with the following terms and conditions.
#
# Permission to copy, modify, and distribute this software and its documentation, with or
# without modification, for any purpose and without fee or royalty is hereby granted,
# provided that you include the following on ALL copies of the software and documentation
# or portions thereof, including modifications:
#
#    1. The full text of this NOTICE in a location viewable to users of the redistributed
#       or derivative work.
#    2. Any pre-existing intellectual property disclaimers, notices, or terms and
#       conditions. If none exist, the W3C Software Short Notice should be included
#       (hypertext is preferred, text is permitted) within the body of any redistributed
#       or derivative code.
#    3. Notice of any changes or modifications to the files, including the date changes
#       were made. (We recommend you provide URIs to the location from which the code is
#       derived.)
#
# THIS SOFTWARE AND DOCUMENTATION IS PROVIDED "AS IS," AND COPYRIGHT HOLDERS MAKE NO
# REPRESENTATIONS OR WARRANTIES, EXPRESS OR IMPLIED, INCLUDING BUT NOT LIMITED TO,
# WARRANTIES OF MERCHANTABILITY OR FITNESS FOR ANY PARTICULAR PURPOSE OR THAT THE USE
# OF THE SOFTWARE OR DOCUMENTATION WILL NOT INFRINGE ANY THIRD PARTY PATENTS,
# COPYRIGHTS, TRADEMARKS OR OTHER RIGHTS.
#
# COPYRIGHT HOLDERS WILL NOT BE LIABLE FOR ANY DIRECT, INDIRECT, SPECIAL OR
# CONSEQUENTIAL DAMAGES ARISING OUT OF ANY USE OF THE SOFTWARE OR DOCUMENTATION.
#
# The name and trademarks of copyright holders may NOT be used in advertising or
# publicity pertaining to the software without specific, written prior permission.
# Title to copyright in this software and any associated documentation will at all
# times remain with copyright holders.
###############################################################################

import   sys
import   time
from      datetime        import   datetime
from      random          import   randint
```

```python
###############################################
# Write timestamped message to log file
def writeLog(logFile, message):

        now = datetime.today().strftime('%Y-%m-%d %H:%M:%S')
        print(now+": "+ str(message) )

        handle = open(logFile,"a")
        handle.write(now+ ": " +str(message)+ "\n")
        handle.close()
#--------------------

###############################################
# Gracefully close the bot
def closeBot(logFile, driver, msg):
        writeLog(logFile, "Shutting down program: " + msg)

        writeLog(logFile, "Closing browser")
        driver.close()

        writeLog(logFile, "Closing Webdriver")
        driver.quit()

        now = datetime.today().strftime('%Y-%m-%d %H:%M:%S')
        writeLog(logFile, "This bot closed at: " + now)
        sys.exit()
#--------------------

###############################################
# Provide a random, logged, delay with countdown to console
def randomWait(logFile, lo, hi):

        # Get random delay time and echo to screen & log
        randomDelay = randint(lo, hi)

        writeLog(logFile, 'Waiting '+str(randomDelay))

        # Provide the actual delay and countdown (on console only)
        now = datetime.today().strftime('%Y-%m-%d %H:%M:%S')
        print(now+": ", end='', flush=True)
        print(str(randomDelay)+", ", end='', flush=True)
        randomDelay = randomDelay -1
        while randomDelay >0:
                time.sleep(1)

                print(str(randomDelay)+", ", end='', flush=True)
                randomDelay -=1

        # print a line feed when done
        print("")

#--------------------
```

280

```
##############################################
# Write data to a file
def writeFile(logFile, fileName, data):

        # Log that the file was written
        writeLog(logFile, "Writing file: " + fileName)

        # Write the file  and close
        f = open(fileName, "w")
        f.write(data)
        f.close()
#--------------------


##############################################
# Append data to the end of a file
def appendFile(logFile, fileName, data):

        # Log that the file was written
        writeLog(logFile, "Appending to file: " + fileName)

        # Write the file  and close
        f = open(fileName, "a")
        f.write(data)
        f.close()
#--------------------


##############################################
# Append data to the end of a file
def getWebpageContents(logFile, driver):

        # Log that webpage was saved to variable
        writeLog(logFile, "Capturing screen contents")

        # Execute Javascript to obtain active web content
        # html = driver.execute_script("return document.body.innerHTML;")
        html = driver.page_source
        return html
#--------------------


##############################################
# Obtain the fully resolved, absolute address for a URL
def getAbsoluteAddress(logFile, driver, href):
        # Log that webpage was saved to variable
        absoluteAddress = driver.execute_script("return (function(relative) { var a =
document.createElement('a'); a.href = relative; return a.href; })(arguments[0])", href);

        return absoluteAddress
#--------------------


##############################################
# Append data to the end of a CSV file
def writeCSV(logFile, filePath, ARRcsv):
```

```
        thisLine = ""
        for data in ARRcsv:
                thisLine = thisLine + '"' + str(data) + '",'

        appendFile(logFile, filePath, thisLine + "\n")
#--------------------

############################################################################
```

4.2 *libParse.py*

```
###############################################################################
#
# libParse.py
#
# From the book: Developing Bots with Selenium Python, @2023 Michael Schrenk
# Usage via the W3C Software Notice and License (below).
#
###############################################################################
# W3C SOFTWARE NOTICE AND LICENSE
# http://www.w3.org/Consortium/Legal/2002/copyright-software-20021231
#
# This work (and included software, documentation such as READMEs, or other
# related items) is being provided by the copyright holders under the following license.
# By obtaining, using and/or copying this work, you (the licensee) agree that you have
# read, understood, and will comply with the following terms and conditions.
#
# Permission to copy, modify, and distribute this software and its documentation, with or
# without modification, for any purpose and without fee or royalty is hereby granted,
# provided that you include the following on ALL copies of the software and documentation
# or portions thereof, including modifications:
#
#    1. The full text of this NOTICE in a location viewable to users of the redistributed
#       or derivative work.
#    2. Any pre-existing intellectual property disclaimers, notices, or terms and
#       conditions. If none exist, the W3C Software Short Notice should be included
#       (hypertext is preferred, text is permitted) within the body of any redistributed
#       or derivative code.
#    3. Notice of any changes or modifications to the files, including the date changes
#       were made. (We recommend you provide URIs to the location from which the code is
#       derived.)
#
# THIS SOFTWARE AND DOCUMENTATION IS PROVIDED "AS IS," AND COPYRIGHT HOLDERS MAKE NO
# REPRESENTATIONS OR WARRANTIES, EXPRESS OR IMPLIED, INCLUDING BUT NOT LIMITED TO,
# WARRANTIES OF MERCHANTABILITY OR FITNESS FOR ANY PARTICULAR PURPOSE OR THAT THE USE
# OF THE SOFTWARE OR DOCUMENTATION WILL NOT INFRINGE ANY THIRD PARTY PATENTS,
# COPYRIGHTS, TRADEMARKS OR OTHER RIGHTS.
#
# COPYRIGHT HOLDERS WILL NOT BE LIABLE FOR ANY DIRECT, INDIRECT, SPECIAL OR
# CONSEQUENTIAL DAMAGES ARISING OUT OF ANY USE OF THE SOFTWARE OR DOCUMENTATION.
#
# The name and trademarks of copyright holders may NOT be used in advertising or
# publicity pertaining to the software without specific, written prior permission.
# Title to copyright in this software and any associated documentation will at all
# times remain with copyright holders.
###############################################################################

import re
#--------------------

#############################################
```

```python
# Define parsing parameters
BEFORE = True
AFTER = False
INCL = True
EXCL = False
#--------------------

##############################################
# Return true/false if needle is in haystack
def stristr(haystack, needle):
        pos = haystack.upper().find(needle.upper())
        if pos < 0: # not found
                return False
        else:
                return True
#--------------------

##############################################
# Strip all tags from returned string
def stripTags(string):
    return re.sub('<[^<]+?>', '', string)
#--------------------

##############################################
# Return string between start and end, INCL/EXCL delimiters
def returnBetween(string, start, end, incl):
        start_index = string.find(start)
        if start_index == -1:
                return ""
        end_index = string.find(end, start_index + len(start))

        if end_index == -1:
                return ""

        if incl:
                return start + string[start_index + len(start):end_index] + end
        else:
                return string[start_index + len(start):end_index]
#--------------------

##############################################
# Returns the subject, where "search" is substituted with "replace"
def strReplace(search, replace, subject):
    return subject.replace(search, replace)
#--------------------

##############################################
# Returns an array containing what's contained by
# repeating open and close tags
def parseArray(string, openTag, closeTag, incl):
    # First, split the string by the open tag
    split_by_open = string.split(openTag)
```

```python
    # Prepare an empty list to hold the results
    results = []

    # Loop through each part
    for part in split_by_open[1:]:  # Skip the first item (before the first open tag)
        # Then split each part by the close tag
        split_by_close = part.split(closeTag, 1)  # Only split at the first close tag

        # The first item in this list is the content between the tags
        content = split_by_close[0]

        # If INCL equals "EXCL", include the delimiters in the result
        if incl:
            content = openTag + content + closeTag

        # Add the content to the results list
        results.append(content)

    # Return the results
    return results
#--------------------

###############################################
# Returns the TITLE from an HTML document
def parsePageTitle(logFile, driver):
        pageTitle =  driver.execute_script("return document.title;")

        return pageTitle
#--------------------

###############################################
# Returns the HEAD from an HTML document
def parsePageHead(logFile, driver):
        pageHead =  driver.execute_script("return document.head.innerHTML;")

        return pageHead
#--------------------

###############################################
# Returns the META DESCRIPTION from an HTML document
def parsePageDescription(logFile, driver):
        head = parsePageHead(logFile, driver)

        ARRmeta = parseArray(head, "<meta", ">")
        for metaTag in ARRmeta:
                if stristr(metaTag, '"description"'):
                        # parse everything between quotes and selarated by commas
                        Description = metaTag.split(",")
                else:
                        Description = "None found"

        return Description
#--------------------
```

```
################################################
# Splits a string at a delimiter, choose before or after
def splitString(input_str, delimiter, before=True, inclusive=False):
    try:
        delim_index = input_str.index(delimiter)
    except ValueError:
        return "Delimiter not found in input string"

    if before:
        if inclusive:
            return input_str[:delim_index+len(delimiter)]
        else:
            return input_str[:delim_index]
    else:
        if inclusive:
            return input_str[delim_index:]
        else:
            return input_str[delim_index+len(delimiter):]
#--------------------


################################################
# Splits the string at the specified index.
# Returns a tuple with the substring before the index and the substring at and after the
index.
def splitStringAtIndex(string, index):
    """
    """
    substring_before = string[:index]
    substring_after = string[index:]
    return substring_before, substring_after
#--------------------


################################################
# Returns a set of keywords found in a HTML document
def parsePageKeywords(logFile, driver):
        head = parsePageHead(logFile, driver)

        ARRmeta = parserray(head, "<meta", ">")
        for metaTag in ARRmeta:
                if stristr(metaTag, '"keywords"'):
                        # parse everything between quotes and selarated by commas
                        keywords = metaTag.split(",")

        ARRcleanDescriptions = []
        try:
                for word in keywords:
                        if stristr(word, "="):
                                # skip, this is a content designation
                                null = 1
                        else:
                                word = word.strip()
                                word = word.strip('"')
```

286

```
                              word = word.strip("'")
                              ARRcleanDescriptions.append(str(word))
        except:
                ARRcleanDescriptions.append("None Found")

        return ARRcleanDescriptions
#--------------------
```

4.3 *LIB*S*ELENIUM.PY*

```
###############################################################################
#
# libSelenium.py
#
# From the book: Developing Bots with Selenium Python, @2023 Michael Schrenk
# Usage via the W3C Software Notice and License (below).
#
###############################################################################
# W3C SOFTWARE NOTICE AND LICENSE
# http://www.w3.org/Consortium/Legal/2002/copyright-software-20021231
#
# This work (and included software, documentation such as READMEs, or other
# related items) is being provided by the copyright holders under the following license.
# By obtaining, using and/or copying this work, you (the licensee) agree that you have
# read, understood, and will comply with the following terms and conditions.
#
# Permission to copy, modify, and distribute this software and its documentation, with or
# without modification, for any purpose and without fee or royalty is hereby granted,
# provided that you include the following on ALL copies of the software and documentation
# or portions thereof, including modifications:
#
#    1. The full text of this NOTICE in a location viewable to users of the redistributed
#       or derivative work.
#    2. Any pre-existing intellectual property disclaimers, notices, or terms and
#       conditions. If none exist, the W3C Software Short Notice should be included
#       (hypertext is preferred, text is permitted) within the body of any redistributed
#       or derivative code.
#    3. Notice of any changes or modifications to the files, including the date changes
#       were made. (We recommend you provide URIs to the location from which the code is
#       derived.)
#
# THIS SOFTWARE AND DOCUMENTATION IS PROVIDED "AS IS," AND COPYRIGHT HOLDERS MAKE NO
# REPRESENTATIONS OR WARRANTIES, EXPRESS OR IMPLIED, INCLUDING BUT NOT LIMITED TO,
# WARRANTIES OF MERCHANTABILITY OR FITNESS FOR ANY PARTICULAR PURPOSE OR THAT THE USE
# OF THE SOFTWARE OR DOCUMENTATION WILL NOT INFRINGE ANY THIRD PARTY PATENTS,
# COPYRIGHTS, TRADEMARKS OR OTHER RIGHTS.
#
# COPYRIGHT HOLDERS WILL NOT BE LIABLE FOR ANY DIRECT, INDIRECT, SPECIAL OR
# CONSEQUENTIAL DAMAGES ARISING OUT OF ANY USE OF THE SOFTWARE OR DOCUMENTATION.
#
# The name and trademarks of copyright holders may NOT be used in advertising or
# publicity pertaining to the software without specific, written prior permission.
# Title to copyright in this software and any associated documentation will at all
# times remain with copyright holders.
###############################################################################

import sys
from selenium import webdriver
from selenium.webdriver.chrome.options import Options
```

```
###############################################
# Establish paths
pathLibs                        = "."

###############################################
# Import local libraries
sys.path.insert(0, pathLibs)
import libBot              # Useful bot functions


###############################################
def setWindowSize(logFile, driver, x, y):
        libBot.writeLog(logFile, "Setting window size to " + str(x) + "px by " + str(y) +
"px.")
        driver.set_window_size(x, y)
#-------------------

###############################################
def setWindowPosition(logFile, driver, x, y):
        libBot.writeLog(logFile, "Positioning window to " + str(x) + ", " + str(y) + ".")
        driver.set_window_position(x, y)
#-------------------

###############################################
def loadWebdriver(logFile, pathChromeDriver):
        options = webdriver.ChromeOptions()
        options.add_argument("--user-agent=Mozilla/5.0 (Windows NT 10.0; Win64; x64)
AppleWebKit/537.36 (KHTML, like Gecko) Chrome/87.0.4280.67 Safari/537.36");
        options.add_argument('ignore-certificate-errors')

        libBot.writeLog(logFile, "Loading chromedriver")
        service = webdriver.chrome.service.Service(executable_path=pathChromeDriver)
        service.start()
        driver = webdriver.Chrome(service=service, options=options)

        return driver
#-------------------

###############################################
def loadHeadlessWebdriver(logFile, pathChromeDriver):
        options = webdriver.ChromeOptions()
        options.add_argument("--user-agent=Mozilla/5.0 (Windows NT 10.0; Win64; x64)
AppleWebKit/537.36 (KHTML, like Gecko) Chrome/87.0.4280.67 Safari/537.36");
        options.add_argument("--headless=new")
        options.add_argument('ignore-certificate-errors')

        libBot.writeLog(logFile, "Loading headless chromedriver")
        service = webdriver.chrome.service.Service(executable_path=pathChromeDriver)
        service.start()
        driver = webdriver.Chrome(service=service, options=options)

        return driver
```

```
#-------------------
```

Section V: Index

www.ingramcontent.com/pod-product-compliance
Lightning Source LLC
LaVergne TN
LVHW081335050326
832903LV00024B/1163